WHY
CULTURE
MATTERS

WHY CULTURE MATTERS

A Biblical Christian approach to things cultural

JOHN NORSWORTHY

Why Culture Matters
Published by ConsultEd Publishing
Tauranga, New Zealand

© 2009 John Norsworthy

ISBN 978-0-473-15764-7 (Softcover)
ISBN 978-0-473-34703-1 (ePub)
ISBN 978-0-473-34704-8 (Kindle)

Distributed by
Castle Publishing Ltd
www.castlepublishing.co.nz

Typesetting & Production:
Andrew Killick
Castle Publishing Services

Cover design:
Paul Smith

I warmly commend this book as a serious introduction to the strategic place of culture in Christian life and service. Its helpful surveys of the way culture functions in Scripture, in the early Christian community and in the historic phases of Christianity lay a solid foundation for wise practical guidance on addressing cultural issues and challenges in our diverse multicultural contexts of the 21ˢᵗ Century.

John Hitchen BA, BD, PhD (Senior lecturer in Mission, Laidlaw College, Auckland, formerly Principal, Bible College of New Zealand, and Christian Leaders' Training College of Papua New Guinea)

A much needed skill in communicating with today's global community is an awareness and appreciation of various cultures. This book is an easy to read primer on Christianity and culture. It can add value to the person seeking to develop in this area. The chapter on "The Contemporary Global Challenge" is a must read for Christian leaders in New Zealand facing fast emerging multicultural congregations.

Andrew Kulasingham (Deputy Principal, Faith Bible College, New Zealand)

Culture is like water to a fish: it surrounds, supports and gives life but is hard to see. In this book John Norsworthy helps us understand culture and how it imposes its unquestioned values upon us. Furthermore this book describes the unique work of Christ in culture and how Christ transcends all man's attempts to define meaning and purpose in life. I commend this very timely and readable work to any student of culture and faith.

Rev. Craig Vernall (Senior Minister, Bethlehem Baptist Church, Tauranga, New Zealand)

May I recommend this well written and readable book to you. It invites you to consider a biblical approach to understanding cultures, since creation to the present day. It traces man's responses to the will of a holy God, and the context and relevance of the times and places in which we find ourselves. John Norsworthy, an experienced educator, raises some fundamental questions and suggests sensible solutions for us in this new century with its multicultural environment. This book will be most helpful to students interested in the development of "culture" through a biblical, Christ-centred lens, and a useful resource for teachers in various contexts.

Graham C Preston (Founder and Ambassador of Christian Education Trust (CET), formerly Principal of Bethlehem College)

Contents

Preface   9
Describing culture   11

CULTURE IN THE OLD TESTAMENT   21
The beginnings of culture   23
Using cultural practices to reveal deeper truth   29
Missing the heart of their God-given culture   37

CULTURE IN THE NEW TESTAMENT   43
The life of Christ and culture   45
The cultural theme of the Book of Acts   53
Cultural freedom and choices in the teaching of Paul   63
The importance of cultural forms   69
Church culture in the New Testament   81
Connecting with the thinking of a Gentile culture   87

CULTURE IN CHURCH HISTORY   93
Christianity in the Roman Empire and Middle Ages   95
The power and vulnerability of the Kingdom   105
Reforming the culture   113
Culture and the modern missionary movement   119

CULTURE IN TODAY'S WORLD   125
Effecting cultural change in the contemporary world   127
Multiculturalism and biculturalism   143
The contemporary global challenge   155

CULTURE FOR ETERNITY   163
The ultimate glorious unity in diversity   165

References   169
About the author   176

Preface

My upbringing was such that whenever I faced a new concept or challenge, I would consciously or sub-consciously ask the question, "What does the Bible say about this?" For some time I have looked for a small text or primer introducing the reader to a biblical approach to things cultural. Eventually, I decided I should write it myself. The intention is that this book could be read and discussed by individuals or classes in a church or school setting.

When I embarked on writing this book I was very much aware that I would not be expounding some new revelation. God has already used others to do that and caused it to be recorded in His Word, the Bible. This book is not the result of some groundbreaking research. I am not an academic or researcher. What I have written has been said by others in various writings and presentations. Indeed there are many books written and messages presented on the various aspects of the biblical truth I am writing about, many by experienced authors and preachers all of whom are far more eloquent than I. What I can contribute is a simple clear way of presenting the ideas so that others may catch the concepts and weave them into their being and so apply them to their life's calling, whether that be evangelism, pastoral and teaching ministry, counselling or any of a vast array of vocations in which Christians find themselves needing to work, including cross-cultural or multicultural contexts.

Some forty years ago, one of my Bible college lecturers wanted to make the course he was presenting as simple and as clear as he could for us to grasp. He effectively summarised the course with four main principles. He was pleased with himself. A short time later he read what St Augustine had written on the topic a millennium and a half earlier. He too summarised the topic with the same four principles. This boosted my lecturer's humility somewhat but in no way reduced his enthusiasm to present the course in this way. The wisdom of Augustine confirmed his approach. If after writing this book I discover someone has already written it, I will still be enthusiastic about it.

This is not a 'how to' text but rather a 'why we should' text – a biblical rationale. If we want to be strategically intentional in shaping the future we need to know not just where we are now, but where we have come from, and where we are ultimately going. We need to know the reason for the journey. It is my intention to briefly sketch the biblical teaching about culture by tracing the theme through the biblical meta-narrative – from Genesis to Revelation via the present.

I have been inspired over the years by those who have written before me. Much of what they have written has become deeply implanted in my understanding. Consequently, as I write from my heart I may well be reflecting these writers and preachers. The first parts of the book consist of a biblical survey in which I have not consciously referred to writers other than those of the scripture, whereas toward the end of the book where I apply biblical principles, I refer to some other writers. The references at the end include the books that I am aware have most influenced my thinking about this theme over the years and in recent months. I wish to honour the authors for their faithfulness in contributing to the work of the Kingdom in their writing. In particular I want to honour the late Dr Glenn Martin who was Chair of Social Sciences at Wesleyan University, Marion, Indiana. He did not publish his work[1] but personally and significantly influenced myself and others on his visits 'down under'. I also wish to thank those who have critiqued drafts of this work, and encouraged me in the process.

To God be the glory.

1. See, Martin, Glenn R. (2006). Prevailing worldviews of western society since 1500. Marion, IN: Triangle Publishing. Some of his work collated and published since his death in 2004.

ONE

Describing Culture

In the 1960s in Australia where I grew up, a young 'bloke' was stereotypically characterised by his affinity to football, meat pies, cars and beer. He was definitely not connected to anything called 'culture'. In that generation 'culture' referred to 'high culture' as distinct from 'popular culture', and anyone who showed some 'culture' was not part of the 'average' man's social set. The meaning of the word 'culture' has changed since those days.

Any number of definitions of 'culture' can be found. Some are terse one-liners. Others are complex and fill many pages of text. Currently, and in this book, 'culture' is used to describe the general concept of the shared ideas and actions found in a subset of humanity. This subset of humanity is typically a people group or 'ethnic' group (from the Greek 'ethnos' meaning a nation or people), but could be a broad sweeping group such as the 'Western world' or as narrow as a small organisation of people such as a family or a school. The group's culture is the generally shared things that they do and the values that engender these shared actions.

I belong to a tennis club. We of course play tennis, sometimes seriously in a competition, but often casually just for the pleasure of the process. We have morning tea together. We celebrate success by awarding prizes to tournament winners. We have excellent artificial surface courts and a clubhouse which consists of change rooms, a kitchen and a large area to sit around tables to eat and chat together, and a bar to serve drinks. We meet for casual tennis on Saturday afternoons and Wednesday mornings, and competitive tennis on Monday nights and at interclub tournaments. These are some of the observable things we do. But there are values which hold us together as a group. We of course all value the game of tennis. We value fair play, encouraging one another, team work, and sincere honest fellowship – we are a very friendly club. The absence of tiered seats to observe the tennis may suggest we value participation more than mere observation of the game. These actions and values are not *equally* shared by all. Some do not come on Wednesdays or play in tournaments. Some do not buy at the bar. Not everyone is equally encouraging. We vary in our competitiveness. But the general pattern is there and serves to define the club's culture.

In schools the concept of cultures is often introduced by describing cultural differences. Invariably, these differences are easily observable things that people do. They include: what, how and when people eat, the buildings in which they live, the way they celebrate and play, their artistic expressions such as their music, dancing and painting, the clothes they wear, greetings, and the way they form and govern relationships. Such phenomena can be generally called cultural forms, and can be the subject of fascinating study and research.

For some, this is as deep as their thinking about culture goes. But beneath the surface of these observable patterns of practice and corporate actions exists a vital inner world of the mind and heart. These are ideas and values which are the source of the words and actions. The patterns of ideas shared by the group are as much a part of the culture as the immediately observable. These shared values often give the group its synergy. Often they are unexamined assumptions, and so may be called, for a lack of a better term, 'common sense'.

This distinction between the observable features of a culture and the not so immediately observed world of thoughts and attitudes is a major theme of this book. For the purpose of the thesis of this book it would be neat to say that these two major aspects of a culture were quite separate. But they are not – they are organically linked. Yet there is a clear distinction between them. The following charts may help the reader understand this distinction.

The nature of the two parts of culture

OUTER CULTURE	INNER CULTURE
External	Internal
Observable	Not immediately observable
Cultural forms	Cultural foundations
Patterns of practice	Patterns of thinking
Expressions of being human	The heart of being human

Fundamental to a culture is the shared language. This includes the broad language form such as Japanese or Spanish, but also the shared idioms, metaphors and subtle nuances which have special meaning to the group. More than anything else, it is the shared language which makes the vital connection between the foundations of the culture and the forms of the culture. Until you understand the language of a culture, it has been said, you have not understood the culture.

What gives a culture its particular shape?

A culture is shaped by various factors. These may be geographical, such as weather patterns or peculiar features of the local terrain. They may be historical, such as the domination of a particular group

The content of the two parts of culture

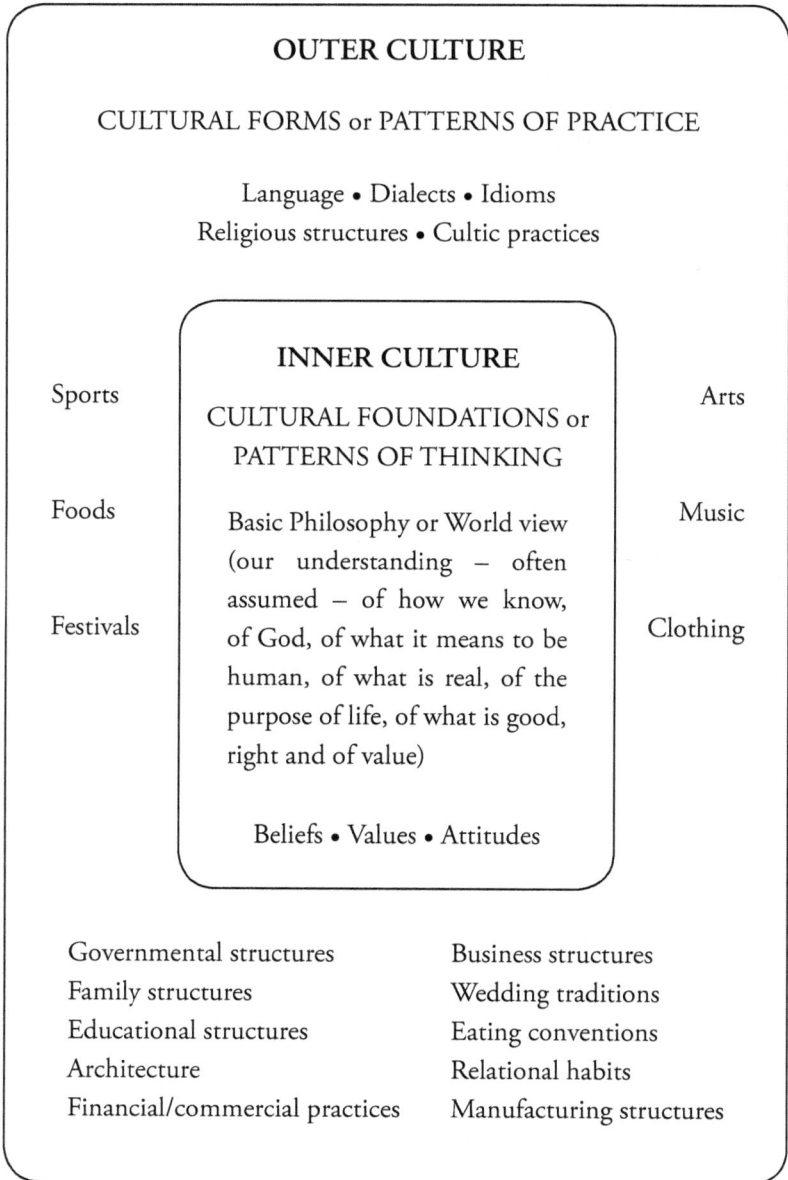

OUTER CULTURE

CULTURAL FORMS or PATTERNS OF PRACTICE

Language • Dialects • Idioms
Religious structures • Cultic practices

Sports

Foods

Festivals

INNER CULTURE

CULTURAL FOUNDATIONS or
PATTERNS OF THINKING

Basic Philosophy or World view (our understanding – often assumed – of how we know, of God, of what it means to be human, of what is real, of the purpose of life, of what is good, right and of value)

Beliefs • Values • Attitudes

Arts

Music

Clothing

Governmental structures   Business structures
Family structures   Wedding traditions
Educational structures   Eating conventions
Architecture   Relational habits
Financial/commercial practices   Manufacturing structures

in a certain era, or the timing of the development of governmental or educational systems. The philosophical understanding of the world held by people in the group, both currently and historically, and whether 'religious' or 'non-religious' have a huge influence on the shaping of the culture. We operate from assumptions held consciously or subconsciously. They have a deep-seated effect on our values and subsequent practices. Such presuppositions provide the foundation for the values found in the culture. Some cultures have been shaped almost exclusively by one religion or worldview. Others, like the cultures of most current Western nations, are shaped by various religions and worldviews.

The derivation of the English words cult, cultivate and culture illustrates the strong connection between religious practices, groups who nurture these practices, and the development of the land, the customs, products and artefacts which are an integral part of these shared activities. In a modern secular setting we tend to underestimate the connection between our deepest convictions and our culture, yet it is the ideas shared at this level which ultimately have shaped and maintain the culture. And it is a change in these ideas that have the potential to transform the culture of a people group, if for no other reason than they give a sense of ultimate value and ultimate transformation.

Cultural differences are not genetically determined. They are shaped by 'enculturation'. Maria grew up in a European family, went to an Anglican church, and lived in a very mono-cultural European city, Christchurch, in New Zealand. She thought like a European and behaved like a European, and identified with European New Zealanders, yet her skin colour was very dark. When people first met her they saw her skin and expected her to think and behave like a Maori. She had very little idea of what *that* way of being would be. Culturally, she was not Maori, racially she was Maori. 'Culture' is not the same as 'race'. Racial differences are biological. Sadly, we somehow make an inordinate distinction between people on the basis of these very minor biological differences. Indeed, because the biological differences *within* a 'race' are far more than those *between* the 'races', we would all do well to be 'colour blind', especially when making initial contact with a stranger. It would certainly help when initially relating to a person like Maria, or the many racially African or Asian people who are part of the mainstream culture of modern Western nations. A challenge for Maria was to answer the question sometimes posed to her on government forms, "What is your ethnicity?" The concept of ethnicity seems to engage both culture and race.

Cultural clashes

Radio receivers exist in an environment of many radio waves. When tuned in they can 'pick up' and transform some of those signals into 'real' sound. Like radios, we catch the presuppositions, values and cultural forms from our family and the culture of our surrounding society.

I grew up in the fifties and sixties. My family (and consequently I) had nothing to do with contemporary 'worldly' music. We experienced the contemporary music styles at a distance. Recently my wife and I enjoyed attending a fifties style rock concert. The lyrics of the songs had no overt connection to our commitment to the Lord. There was nothing explicitly Christian about the concert. But we enjoyed the music simply because its style was the style of music we heard when we were children and teenagers. Heaps of 'oldies' like us were there enjoying it, presumably for the same sorts of reasons. We reflected on how we did not actively participate in this music as young people, yet, at the level of our 'natural' minds, we probably enjoyed the concert far more than we would a contemporary concert – even a Christian contemporary music concert. As we grow older we realise that the cultural forms we experienced repeatedly in our formative years become imprinted on our consciousness in such a way that they become attached to us.

One of the things we tend to do when we are under pressure or when we are suffering trauma is to revert to the safety of familiar people, familiar ideas and familiar cultural forms. For example, my wife points out to me that when I am nervous I sing or whistle old (and sometimes totally antiquated) familiar songs.

If these cultural forms of our youth have connection to values we were taught there is a good chance we will hold on to those values as well. We tend to absorb presuppositions and values subconsciously, especially in our youth. As we become adults we develop the ability to examine these assumptions. I am encouraged when I see adolescents questioning and making a conscious effort to accept or reject these ideas. I am discouraged when I see adults unable to work through this process with them. Unless as adults we are careful to think this process through, we miss out on the privilege of choosing the best presuppositions and values for ourselves and of guiding our children through the same process. If we have not consciously chosen our presuppositions and values we effectively are entrapped by them. The unexamined life is a blinkered life. It is an unwitting narrow-mindedness. It is a form of cultural acquiescence. We become slaves of the ideas that have captured our minds.

As a result of this preference for the familiar, we can assign inordinate value to some cultural forms, simply because we feel comfortable with them, and depreciate other cultural forms because they are not familiar to us. Thus a cultural difference between 'us' and 'them' can become a 'cultural gap'. Such a cultural gap may be related to ethnicity, age, or social status. This can escalate. Selective value judgment attached to cultural forms may lead to a 'clash of cultures'. Language barriers can compound the problem, particularly since our communication is culturally interpreted. Derogatory terms such as 'racist' or 'ageist' can get thrown into the fray. When such selective judgment is shared by the group, whether family or nation, it can very easily lead to a feud or war. The justification (conscious or otherwise) of the conflict is the protection and preservation of the culture. Some such recent conflicts have been described as 'ethnic cleansing'. The book will return to discuss these issues in the light of the gospel of Christ later in the book.

Before beginning a survey of the scripture, it is helpful to allude to the role of culture in the writing and subsequent interpretation of scripture. The authors of scripture, those whom God inspired, lived in a specific place, time and culture. To interpret his message we need to consider the cultural setting of the author and of his first audience. Sometimes the message of a certain passage unambiguously transcends the cultural setting, but we cannot assume this. To ignore the cultural background can lead to an incorrect interpretation of the text. If we ignore it, we will most likely interpret the passage through the filter of our own culture. This could produce a strange warping of the truth.

So what does the Bible say?

To study and discuss

1. Classify the following as a cultural form or a cultural foundation (it may take some discussion to arrive at some consensus): Belief in God, Football, Shame and honour, Democracy, A free media, Nudity and clothing, The last rites, Gentleness of spirit, The value of human life, The education system, The law against murder, Monogamy, Rock music.

2. Have you examined your family's culture?
Describe it in terms of its:
- Cultural forms – The way you eat, the way you celebrate, the way you relate, the things you do together...
- Values – What values hold you together? What about your family history is a valued story? Is there a valued common interest, activity or sport?
- Basic 'presuppositions' – Do you share beliefs which answer questions such as "Who are we as humans?", "What or Who is real and true?" and "How do we know what is true?"

How have you been encouraged to examine these basic 'presuppositions?'

3. What cultural forms are you aware of that you enjoy?
What is your attitude to people who enjoy different cultural forms?
What do you do if other cultural forms make you feel uncomfortable?
How do you feel about people whose basic presuppositions (beliefs) are different to yours?

CULTURE IN THE OLD TESTAMENT

TWO

The Beginnings of Culture

It begins with God. The word for God in the very first verse of the Bible is a plural word – a bit like the word 'trousers', plural but describing a unity. It indicates God is diverse in His[2] unity. He said, "Let *us* create man in *our* image".[3] In creating us in His image, he planned for us to be diverse, just as plurality is part of His very nature. He made us male and female to enable a diverse population. Sexual reproduction enables humans to be different from each other yet at the same time to share our common humanity.

God's original work for the human race was for us to reflect God's Lordship over His creation by 'taking dominion' over the earth.[4] Some translations of Genesis read 'cultivate' the earth. As faithful stewards, we were instructed to manage (develop and conserve) the resources of the planet, listening intently to the voice of God as we went about the task. God told us to reproduce ourselves and fill the earth to achieve this 'cultural commission'. In this way we would each reflect differently the character of God while working together in cooperation with Him. We would each play a different part in fulfilling the task God has given us, this 'cultural commission'. Every imaginable vocation (not involving sin)

---

2. I use the traditional masculine pronouns when referring to God because of the lack in the English language of a neutral personal pronoun. God of course transcends sexuality and gender identity.

3. Genesis 1:26

4. Genesis 1:26-28

is needed to develop and conserve the earth. In this sense we were created cultural beings – each one of us contributing to human culture using the unique gifts with which God has graced us. We were made to be diverse people in diverse places. This diversity is an integral part of God's original plan for us. It is one way in which we can manifest different dimensions of the diversity found in God himself.

The effect of the fall

The first humans did not keep to doing everything God's way. They chose to disobey God. They fell short of God's perfect plan. We call this 'the fall'.[5]

The fall of the human race caused a fundamental change in the nature of the way in which human culture would unfold. As promised, death came into the human race through the fall. There was physical death which became manifest years later. But there was an immediate death. It was the death of the close relationship between God and humans. It was a death in the inside world of humanity. It was a death right at the very foundation of culture. It was this death that poisoned the attitudes of humanity. It was this death which spawned the raft of false ideas about the nature of reality, about the purpose of life, about human values and ambitions. It was this death which led to the other death, the death of the body. Death of the inner person led to corruption of its expression in outward human behaviour and in the constructs of human culture. It was this death which denied us the ability to be good stewards of the world in the context of a dynamic relationship with God.

This spiritual death did not stop the urge to take dominion of the earth, but it reoriented the focus of human endeavour. Instead of human culture being directed toward the glory of God, it

---

5. Read Genesis 3

became focused on the glory of man.[6] Listening to the voice of God to obtain the blueprints for development projects was cast aside. Instead of cultural projects being birthed out of the will of God, they became expressions of defiance against God.

The curse of sin as described in Genesis 3 involved such things as difficulties in parenthood, male chauvinism and difficulties in fulfilling the cultural work we were to do. Adam's and Eve's first diagnosis of the problem was to observe an outward phenomenon. They were naked. And so their first attempt to solve the problem of their guilt was addressing an outward issue. They tried fig leaves, an abysmal failure.[7] Ever since, humans have avoided the real issue in the heart and have made 'fig leaf' attempts to solve the human dilemma.

Not only had they lost their relationship to Him, but future generations were barely aware of His being, let alone His character of justice, faithfulness and love. They were separated from even the knowledge of Him. As the apostle Paul describes it, human culture became characterised by wickedness, evil, greed, depravity, envy, murder, strife, deceit and malice.[8]

Diversity, not conformity

Genesis chapter 10 celebrates the diverse families descended from Noah, each to be different and in different lands as distinct people groups. But they resisted God and worked toward cultural centralisation and conformity. Conformity and control, empire building is not God's plan. So God struck a most effective blow to their plans. The Lord diversified their language.[9] Because language is pivotal to

---

6. I have deliberately used the masculine word man here as the hegemony of men over women is part of the curse of sin, Genesis 3:16
7. Genesis 3:7
8. Romans 1:18-32
9. Genesis 11

the coherence of a cultural group, this forced the issue. It caused geographical separation and so precipitated the cultural diversity now seen between different people groups.

Now they were both separated from God and separated from each other. As was God's plan they developed different cultural forms. But many of these patterns of word and action expressed more and more the depravity of the heart.[10] They resorted to worshiping diverse objects which became significant cultural artefacts. These gods became the focal point of their communities' culture. Subsequent tribal wars became seen as the clash of the tribal gods.

The problem was not their diversity. This was God's original plan for humanity. It was their separation from God. Their diversity, instead of being a beautiful expression of God's glory, became a justification of the ugliness stemming from their separation from God. Unity in diversity is only possible in relationship with God.

---

10. Romans 1:18-32

To study and discuss

1. What vocations are involved in the fulfillment of the cultural commission?

2. Do you see your work as your part in fulfilling the cultural commission or as a necessary drudgery – as it became after the fall?

3. What unique gifts do you have to contribute to human culture?

4. How can you use your gifts to glorify God rather than your own ego?

5. How comfortable are you with the idea that cultural diversity was God's idea?

6. How is God glorified better by there being many ethnic groups?

7. List some of the reasons why cultures clash.

THREE

Using Cultural Practices to Reveal Deeper Truth

Humanity needed to be restored to a right relationship with God. God began by progressively revealing Himself to humanity. He started by appearing in a vision to someone who would choose to believe Him. His name was Abram. He promised to bless Abram by making him the father of not just one family but of a variety of nations. His descendants would be diverse.[11]

One branch of Abram's family was to become a special nation. This selection of one nation was not an act of divine racism. The end purpose was to redeem equally people of all ethnic groups. Abram's descendants were to bless all nations – to teach the nations. This initial educational process was not possible with various people scattered across a range of people groups. Abram's descendants were to become a people group who would adopt a culture stemming out of an understanding of God's message. His message was about His person and character, about their sin, about the nature of God's salvation and about their inability to save themselves. They were to learn that they were in desperate need of a Saviour.

God used existing cultural forms to make the recipients of His message connect with the lesson to be learned. Then He followed up the message with new patterns of practice which served to reinforce the message and to be a tool for educating the next generation in the message.

---

11. Genesis 12:1-3, Genesis 15:1-6

CULTURE AS CONNECTOR	THE LESSON LEARNED	CULTURE AS EDUCATOR
God connects with the patriarchs using existing cultural forms	Lessons about the person, character and purpose of God, and their response to: believe, love and obey God	God adapts cultural practices to apply the lesson and communicate it to the next generation

Abram had occasion to rescue his nephew, Lot, from some Canaanite kings. As a result he gained a considerable amount of goods. It was a pattern of practice to give a portion of your income to the priests of your tribal god. Abram had left his 'tribal' city and was living in Canaan. Melchizedek, the priest of El, the most high God of the Canaanites, came to Abram and blessed him saying, "Blessed be Abram by God Most High, Creator of heaven and earth. And blessed be God Most High, who delivered your enemies into your hand." Thus God prompted Abram to pay tithes to Melchizedek. This familiar cultural form was used as an act of thanksgiving for the Lord's provision.[12]

God changed Abram's name to Abraham, meaning father of nations, to signify his promised patriarchal position. God told Abraham and his male offspring to be circumcised to signify their covenant relationship with God.[13] God's teaching method involved instructing Abram to respond with cultural forms which expressed his committed relationship to Him.

As the story of God's progressive revelation to Israel unfolded we see further cultural forms being used to make connection in the minds of God's people with the lesson He was teaching. For example, when God first confronted Moses with the burning bush,

12. Genesis 14
13. Genesis 17

He instructed him to take off his sandals.[14] Using a cultural custom with which Moses was familiar, God taught him that where He was manifesting His presence was to be recognised as especially holy.

The law of Moses - cultural forms and inner intent

Soon was to follow the institution of the Passover festival, the Sabbath day, and then all the laws established for Israel at Mount Sinai. These patterns of practice included special holy days (holidays), various sacrifices, mediatory professionals (priests), special sacred space (the 'tabernacle'), washing rituals, food laws, how to deal with immorality, crime and infectious diseases, inheritance patterns, property laws and many more. Each of these contributed to the protection and organisation of the people to expedite the purposes of God with Israel. And at the same time they educated the people about who God is and what God had done, and foreshadowed what He planned to do through Christ. Thus God instituted cultural forms which not only would become a means of organising the structure of Israelite society, but also revealed a deeper understanding of Himself, His purposes and the nature of His plan of redemption.

Some critics antagonistic to the biblical story have hastened to claim that the cultural forms of ancient Israel, such as the sacrifices and the temple and its forerunner the 'tabernacle' were very similar to the cultic practices of other Middle Eastern peoples. They claim that the Israelite religion was just another superstitious religion. Indeed, they were very similar, because they were by and large derived from the cultures of the people of the Middle East at that time. When you want to communicate with a group of ancient Middle Easterners, you don't use, say, Chinese symbols or English idioms. God used the cultural forms that they would understand.

---

14. Exodus 3

The critical discernment is not how they were similar, but how, in their similarity, they were radically different.

For example, a major difference was that none of these forms, whether the altar of incense, the sacrificial lamb, the priest, or the Ark of the Covenant, was sacred in itself. The very first of the commandments categorically forbade the creation of anything that would be an object of worship. God and God alone was to be worshiped as holy. The mercy seat above the Ark of the Covenant was only holy in the sense that God manifested His presence there. Unlike the gods of the other people, gods who were part of the creation and indeed created by the people, the God of Israel was truly holy. He was totally other than His creation.

Time is part of God's creation and so no time is divine. The Sabbath was not holy in itself. It was a day set apart to relax, to reflect on who is eternally holy. Unlike the holy days of the other peoples, the special times in the Hebrew calendar were not sacred in themselves. They were set apart to remind them of special milestones in their history, so they would tell their children about who God is and what He had done.

Similarly, the Levitical priests were not holy in themselves. In no sense were they divine. Instead, they were mere humans set apart for their special function in Hebrew society.

The layout of the 'tabernacle' and then the temple, the festivals, and all the cultic practices were symbolic not divine. They were a teaching tool, a shadow of the deeper meaning, not the reality itself. God instituted these forms to reveal the inner truth. It was the deep culture, the mindset of the culture which stood in stark contrast to the worldviews of the surrounding cultures.

As the Israelites moved away from Egypt, God led them through desert. Scary stuff! Where were they going to get food? They needed thousands of tons of it! God said He wanted to test their obedience, because He was about to give them a whole system of laws to live by. He said He would give them food that would literally drop out of the sky overnight and be supplemented with quails in the evening. They were told to gather just enough for each day, no more. On the sixth day of the week they needed to collect a double amount as there would be none on the seventh day when they were to rest.

The first morning they saw this unfamiliar stuff and said "What is it?" So they called it "What is it", manna. They collected and measured it each day and found they had just enough. Some thought they could be clever and collect a double amount to save the work on the next day. Of course this was stealing some other family's meal! But it didn't work. It went rotten overnight. They kept their misdemeanour to themselves. Now when it came to the sixth day they figured that it was pointless gathering a double portion. Wrong again! This time it didn't go rotten and there was nothing on the ground for them the next day. So they went hungry or had to let on that they had disobeyed and proceed to scrounge for food.

God was teaching them to keep the Sabbath. In the process He was educating them about its intent. It was to be on the last day of the week. The week's work had to be done first. Then they could truly relax. They could only truly relax and enjoy it if they first trusted and obeyed Him. You can't enter into Sabbath rest if you don't first trust God. Then, after He instituted the priesthood and the sacrificial system, He taught them that everything that needed to be done on that day to rightly relate to Him was being done in the tabernacle. They just needed to trust and rest.

What brilliant teaching methods! Not only were *they* educated, but thousands of years later, we who believe in Christ and read this story can learn much about entering into the rest Christ has provided for us. To gain an appreciation of the educational role of such cultural forms, I recommend a study of the Jewish Passover meal. The interaction of the father with the family to tell the story of what God did in the exodus and to inculcate attitudes is indeed inspiring.

These cultural forms encoded in laws were not an end in themselves, but were to be the way they outworked their understanding of God and their commitment to Him. The people were to first love God with all their being. The patterns of life were to be an expression of what was in the heart.[15] The truth was to be captured in the mind and enacted with the life.

---

15. Deuteronomy 6

To study and discuss

1. Read some of the book of Leviticus (e.g. chapters 1-5 or chapters 24, 25). Imagine you can be transported in time and place to a family of Levites in the Israelite community at this time.

- Given the cultural forms you have experienced and are comfortable with how do you think you would fit into Israelite society?
- Would you be tempted to use your feelings of discomfort to call the culture sinister?
- Imagine and try to describe and discuss with each other how you would feel having to assimilate into the culture.
- Now, if you were to take an Israelite back with you to your church's Sunday morning service, how do you think they would cope and feel about it?

2. Choose a pattern of practice prescribed by God in the law of Israel and then outline the lessons they would have learned from their practice.

3. Read about the details of the Seder, the Jewish Passover meal and attend a Christian enactment of it.

FOUR

Missing the Heart of their God-given Culture

How were future generations of the people going to appropriate the Law of Moses? They had no king to enforce the law and defend the nation – and fleece them of taxes to do it. The local priests supported by tithes carried out their duties in the community. But every community was left to do what was right in their own eyes, whether informed by the law or otherwise.[16] Some generations failed to pass God's law on to their children and so through lack of knowledge they drifted into a state of apostasy.[17] But on the other hand, when applied, the Law of Moses worked effectively in Israel.

Immigration - choosing to live in a different culture

Ruth lived in Moab. Her husband's parents, Elimelech and Naomi had come from Bethlehem in Judah, part of Israel. Elimelech and Naomi's two sons married Moabite girls, Ruth and Orpah. Then misfortune befell them. All three men died and the three women, Naomi, Orpah and Ruth found themselves bereft of assets, family and hence income. Moab had a king (to tax them) but no welfare system. Naomi knew that Israel had no national government but did have a very workable welfare system. There was provision in the law for widows, orphans, foreigners, and the poor. Families were to fol-

---

16. Judges 21:25
17. Judges 2:7ff

low kinship rules that applied when there was death and misfortune. For aliens, there were hospitality rules that were to be followed. There were rules about local communities enabling the poor to help themselves. Clearly, for Naomi, Israel had a better culture, and the famine which caused them to leave Judah a decade before was over. So she decided to return to the safety of the familiar culture in Bethlehem.

But for the two daughters, Moab with its culture was their native land. On Naomi's advice Orpah returned to her parents' family, but Ruth chose differently. She was very much attached to Naomi, and so was determined to go with her. "Don't urge me to leave you, or to turn back from you. Where you go I will go, and wherever you stay, I will stay. Your people will be my people, and your God, my God..."[18]

On returning to Bethlehem, the citizens of Bethlehem enthusiastically accepted them into the community. Naomi clearly explained to them their bitter experience in Moab. Ruth took advantage of the rules about the poor people gleaning from the harvest. She chose the field of a rich kinsman, Boaz. Boaz treated her very favourably and the story unfolds that, prompted by the God-given cultural rules of kinship, he married her. Ruth became an honoured matriarch in the nation of Israel, the great-grandmother of King David.[19] This resulted from Ruth choosing not only to benefit from the cultural forms of Israel, but also to commit herself to the foundations of that culture. She chose to adopt Naomi's God as her God and the culture which stemmed out of an understanding of Him and His ways.

Worship - with contemporary expression

Since the time of Moses the centre of the worship of God was the 'tabernacle' or tent of meeting. It housed various pieces of furniture

---

18. Ruth 1:16,17
19. In the time between Ruth and David, Israel chose to establish a monarchy.

each of which had a role in the cultic practices of the priesthood. The centre piece was the Ark of the Covenant, above which God manifest His presence – observed only once a year by the high priest on the Day of Atonement. The whole deal – its architecture, its layout, the procedures involved in its use – was established by God hundreds of years before the time of David. God had clearly manifested His presence there and blessed its use. The process had been followed faithfully for generations.

But the Ark had been stolen by the Philistines. The people of Israel had recovered it. It had a hazardous and dramatic journey back to Israel. Someone touched it and consequently died, and it remained in a private home for a period of time. But the day had come to bring the Ark into the newly conquered city of Jerusalem.

King David was really excited about this momentous occasion. The Ark of God was to be once again in the centre of God's people. He had organised the involvement of many people to help make this a great occasion. There was to be a procession accompanying the Ark with all sorts of musical instruments being played. Such musical performance was not prescribed in the Law of Moses. After the Ark had been moved six paces, David made a special sacrifice to the Lord. Then without wearing his kingly regalia, but rather a basic undergarment, a linen ephod, he danced before the Lord with great enthusiasm. With more shouting and trumpet music, David and all the people brought the Ark into Jerusalem. Then the Ark was placed in a tent that David had had erected for it. This was not the traditional 'tabernacle' but a contemporary style tent. Then all the people went home with some bread, meat and raisin cakes.[20]

The whole process was exciting and glorifying to God. But not everyone was happy. One of David's wives, Michal, the daughter of Saul, saw David publicly leaping and whirling in his ephod and deeply despised him. She sarcastically pointed out to him his

20. 2 Samuel 6

indignity. Michal disapproved, but it is not recorded that God did. David was expressing his joy that God was being glorified by this process. Apparently not concerned about the break from the traditional cultural forms, David wanted to resonate with God's pleasure in this occasion. David focused on his relationship with God. He followed the law faithfully, recognising the heart of the law being his love of God.

The heart of the revelation of God – in this case symbolised by the Ark – was not to be touched, but the cultural forms in which it was celebrated and housed were not specific. David revelled in contemporary expression of the inner intent of God's Law.

Culture in decay - missing the original purpose

Far too often in the latter history of the kingdom of Israel and Judah the people failed to follow God with their hearts, and did not subsequently obey His law. Prophets encouraged the people to return to the heart of the law, to repent of their injustice and to love God once again.[21] The prophets would condemn their religious practice, not because the practices were wrong in themselves – God had instituted them – but because they had been disconnected from the truth and attitudes at the heart of the practice.

Some prophets understood God's multi-ethnic purposes and prophesied to the nations. Jonah did not appreciate God's heart for people of all ethnic groups. He struggled with the idea of foreign people responding to the prophetic message, even when he saw that they clearly did. He only saw God's purposes and reputation being intact in the cultural setting that God had shaped in Israel. He failed to see God's inner intent and greater purpose. The book of Jonah describes God's dealings with him so that he would appreciate that His heart is for the welfare of all people.

---

21. e.g. Isaiah 1:11-17, Isaiah 58, Amos 5, Micah 6

When the nation of Israel lost a grip on God's revelation through Moses, the culture fell into disarray. Sometimes a rediscovery of the scripture led to a reformation. But more often God had to raise up prophets to condemn their patterns of practice – institutionalised injustice and corruption. Eventually, Israel and Judah were overtaken by the foreign powers of the day.

At the time of the captivity of the nation of Judah, God encouraged the Jews, through the words of Jeremiah, to settle in Babylon, build houses and gardens to carry on life in this new context, and pray for the prosperity of Babylon, because He had a future plan for them as a nation.[22] This often quoted promise of hope and a future was a charge to engage in the cultural context in which they found themselves, in the light of a future purpose for the nation. It was a challenge to live out their personal days in Babylon while not allowing Babylon to live in them. The life of Daniel exemplified how to do this.[23] Without being judgmental he made a stand – negotiating to not make personal compromises. He was prepared to be civilly disobedient when it was a matter of the heart – his relationship with God. He did not isolate himself from the foreign culture but worked in the Babylonian system, and blessed Babylon with the fruit of his work.

The generations of Jews that followed their return from exile became very more zealous to not fail as the nation had previously done. But on the whole it appears they focused on the forms of the law rather than its intent. They missed the principles of faith, love and the broader purpose of redeeming the nations. They made Jewish cultural forms the centre of their holiness. It was into this scene that Jesus came.

---

22. Jeremiah 29
23. See the story in the book of Daniel

To study and discuss

1. Make a list of cultural practices described in the book of Ruth:
- Discuss how they may have been an outworking of faith and love.
- What equivalent practice is found or could be found in your culture?

2. Select at least one of these passages from the prophets:

Isaiah 1:11-17
Isaiah 58
Amos 5:21-27 (read the beginning of the chapter to get the context)
Micah 6

- What religious practices did God object to?
- Why was He displeased with them?
- What did the prophet say they should be doing?

CULTURE IN THE NEW TESTAMENT

FIVE

The Life of Christ and Culture

Jesus was on His way from Galilee to Jerusalem. Unlike most Jews doing this trip, who would avoid travelling through Samaria, He would at times go straight through the middle and what's more relate to the locals who were partly of a different culture. As He and His disciples were approaching a town on the border of Galilee and Samaria, they were approached by ten men who had skin infections, presumably leprosy. Leprosy is a highly infectious disease. In Israel lepers were usually isolated from the rest of the community by being exiled to outside the town. The men stood at a distance and called out loudly, "Jesus, Master, have pity on us!" On seeing them He said, "Go, show yourself to the priests." This was the requirement of Jewish law. It was the priests' job to check on their health and declare them infectious or not. Jesus encouraged them to obey the rules. On their way to the priests their skin became clean. One of them, when he saw that he was healed, came back, vociferously praised God and thanked Jesus. Jesus said, "Were not all ten cleansed? Where are the other nine? Was no-one found to return and give praise to God except this foreigner? Rise and go; your faith has made you well."[24]

Of all the things He could have said to this man, Jesus highlighted two notable things: The grateful one was a Gentile, and it was not just his actions but his faith – the faith that provoked the

---

24. Luke 17:11-19

obedience – that made him well. Read on, and you will see how these two points are significant.

Keeping the law - incarnation at work

When God came to humanity as a human He came to save all the nations, but He did not come to China, India or Celtic Western Europe. It was necessary for Him to come to a people who had some extra understanding of who God is, of the fallen-ness of humanity, of their desperate need of redemption, and of the nature of that redemptive process. That expresses in essence the purpose of His revelation to ancient Israel, the story of which is recorded in the Old Testament.

Jesus lived his life in Israel. His whole life was lived in Israel, apart from a few months during his infancy when the family were in Egypt, most likely in a Jewish enclave, and an odd excursion to neighbouring Phoenicia. He grew up in a thoroughly Jewish cultural setting. His family was devoutly Jewish. His home town was Jewish. His education was set in this family, town and the local synagogue. He lived as an adult surrounded by Jews. He did things the Jewish way. It is simply erroneous to emphasise the conflicts he had with the culture in which he lived to conclude that He and His followers advocated the abandonment of Jewish culture.

The gospels were written primarily for an audience in a Greek cultural setting. In the case of Matthew it was a mixed (Jewish and Gentile) audience primarily outside of Palestine. It would have been counter-productive to the communication of the story to over-emphasise the Jewishness of the life of Christ, yet the gospels tell of Him doing things the Jewish way. For example, He attended the synagogue on the Sabbath, He celebrated the Passover, He wore Jewish clothing, He gave thanks and blessed food in a Jewish way, and He instructed others to follow the Jewish purity laws.[25] Had He broken Jewish law in a serious way, His critics would not have bothered to draw attention to comparative minor breaches of, for example, Sabbath laws. He kept the Law perfectly. It was essential to the purpose of His incarnation to indwell the culture of the people with whom He came to live.

Not only did He follow the theology and values at the base of Jewish culture but He complied with the cultural forms of the Law of Moses. He did not need to preface His actions with "Moses says do this so I do it". He just did it. He categorically refuted the idea of abolishing the Law of Moses in any way,[26] but instead said He came to fulfil the Law and thus for those who believed in Him, the law would assume a new place and role.

Jesus' approach to Jewish culture

Jesus had created an enormous amount of interest. Crowds were being attracted by His miracles and were listening to His teaching. A delegation of experts, scribes and Pharisees, came to Galilee to observe and discuss issues they had with Him. When they saw some of His disciples eat without first going through the normal religious washing procedures according to the added traditions of the Jewish elders, they were critical. The discussion which ensued, recorded in Mark chapter 7 is an apt illustration of Jesus' approach to Jewish law and custom.

Doing the will of the Father

He practised neither cultural autonomy (independence of the culture) nor cultural acquiescence (unquestioning submission to the

25. e.g. Luke 17:14
26. Matthew 5:17-20

culture). A better way to describe His approach to the Law and its cultural forms is that He did what the Father told Him to do. God had spoken through Moses and confirmed it through the Spirit, and He obeyed the Father. He explained his life choices in these terms.[27] So, not surprisingly, He immediately refers to scripture – what does God say?

Attitude of heart

Quoting Isaiah – "These people honour me with their lips, but their hearts are far from me"[28] – Jesus spoke of the inner intent of the heart being what God sees. It is the immorality that proceeds out of evil intent which defiles a person. This is a major theme of the Sermon on the Mount recorded in Matthew 5-8. It's attitude, attitude, attitude. Hating a person, wanting them dead is as defiling as actually murdering them. Lusting after another person's spouse is as defiling as actually committing adultery.

Priority of God's Word

Jesus always considered the priority of the Torah, the Law of Moses, over subsequent Jewish tradition. For example, the Torah addressed direct contact with sources of contamination. Subsequent Jewish tradition insists on elaborate details of washing of hands before meals to avoid even indirect contact with contamination. Jesus pointed out that these traditions sometimes necessitated the break-ing of the Law of Moses. Obeying God took priority over man-made traditions.[29]

---

27. e.g. John 5:16ff, John7:17ff, John8:25-29
28. Mark 7:6, Isaiah 29:13
29. Mark 7:7-9, Isaiah 29:13

Fulfilling the inner intent

Jesus insisted that the principles behind the details have greater weight. Following the detailed instructions of the law should not hinder exercising faithfulness, justice, mercy and faith. The law was instituted with a view to the fulfilment of these principles in relationship with God. If to fulfil the heart of the law an added detail has to be contravened, so be it. For example, if an act of showing love to people in need of food or healing is contrary to the detailed regulations about keeping the Sabbath, then the regulations are inappropriate. The Sabbath is not holy in itself, but He is holy. He is Lord of the Sabbath.[30]

Raising the bar

When speaking of the moral demands of God, He raised the bar. The heart needs to be right. It is not good enough to just fulfil what the law requires you to do. Our hearts should be set on the righteousness of God. It is not good enough to go along with the law concerning divorce. Our hearts should be set on God's ideal – lifelong faithfulness.[31] There is no room for antinomianism, rejection of the Law, but rather our righteousness should exceed the righteousness of the pedantic scribes and Pharisees. [32]

The law of love

Jesus fulfilled the law as an act of encouragement to obedience. Knowing others were watching him, He did not want to cause them to stumble. He paid the temple tax, not out of obligation but

---

30. Matthew 12:1-14, Luke 6:1-11
31. Matthew 5:31, Matthew 19:1-10, Mark 10:1-12
32. Matthew 5:17-20

so that He did not cause offence.[33] The essence of the Law can be summed up in the principle of loving God and loving others, not in submission to human constructs. Love was more important than all the burnt offerings.[34]

Engaging those of different cultures

Consistent with the purpose of revealing the purpose of His mission to people who had already received the former revelation of God, His ministry was largely with Jews. But He positioned Himself in Galilee, not Judea, for much of it. Here He deliberately came in contact with Gentiles from Syria, Decapolis and Phoenicia. He chose to travel through Samaria sometimes. He surprised the woman at Sychar by talking to her about the things of God.

On one occasion, He deliberately went down to the coast in Phoenicia.[35] A Canaanite woman came to them to seek help for her daughter. The disciples urged Him to send her away. But He refused to do this. He said to them "I was sent only to the lost sheep of Israel." He proceeded to insinuate that she was a Gentile dog. This seems contradictory to His previous actions. Either He was expressing that His main ministry was to Jews or that the lost sheep of the house of Israel included Gentiles, or the more likely interpretation is that he was teaching His disciples with the use of a satirical quoting of a typical Jewish attitude. Whichever way we interpret this comment, the ensuing conversation with her and the healing of her daughter showed that He intentionally extended His ministry to Gentiles.

In summary, we can say that Jesus generally conformed to the culture in which He lived. To do otherwise would have been contrary to the whole principle of His incarnation. He came to be

33. Matthew 17:24-27
34. Mark 12:33
35. Matthew 15:21-28

human, live as a human, identify with humans and communicate with humans. Identifying with the culture is a prerequisite to communicating with the people of the culture.

He particularly followed the customs which expressed the inner intent of the Law. He applauded the aspects of the culture which were an outworking of love.

But where it mattered, He confronted the culture. He spoke against attitudes and acts which were the antithesis of love – evil thoughts, adulteries, fornications, murders, thefts, covetousness, wickedness, deceit, licentiousness, an evil eye, blasphemy, pride, foolishness.[36] He supported the latter prophets' polemic against Israel and Judah in this regard. In no way was the inner intent of the Law to be violated. Offending the heart of the Law was offending God.

He spoke up against obeisance to cultural forms rather than God. He spoke against a lack of integrity – hypocrisy. He spoke up against judgmental attitude. He pointed out that God is Judge, not us. If we judge others, we are setting ourselves up to be judged likewise.[37] He was particularly critical of the religious leaders who judged others on the basis of the cultural forms which had been enshrined in legal traditions.

He lived and ministered in a Jewish culture but reached out to Gentiles when He met them, meeting them where they were geographically and culturally.

And finally His last words with His disciples were a confirmation of the ultimate purposes of His selection of the Jewish nation. He reiterated the blessing of all nations in Abram by commissioning His apostles to make disciples of all nations.[38]

---

36. Mark 7:21,22
37. Matthew 7:1ff
38. Matthew 28:19, Mark 16:15, Luke 24:47, Acts 1:8.

To study and discuss

1. Make a list of teachings recorded in the Sermon on the Mount in Matthew 5-7. (Or in a group discussion, assign a paragraph to each of the group members.) Discuss how in each Jesus:
- Did not advocate breaking the law
- Emphasized the inner intent of the law
- Raised the bar of righteousness

2. Read Matthew 23 in a paraphrase such as *The Message*. Consider it in the light of forms versus foundations, and then attempt to summarise the gist of Jesus' criticism in three short sentences.

3. How many incidences can you find in the gospels where Jesus related meaningfully to and honoured Gentiles?

SIX

The Cultural Theme of the Book of Acts

Luke says right at the beginning of the book of Acts that his gospel, the book of Luke, relates something of what Jesus began to do and teach. The implication is that Acts continues to relate the work of Christ – what Jesus continued to do and teach. So instead of being dubbed the Acts of the Apostles it could be called the continued Acts of Jesus Christ. But then again, the huge emphasis on the work of the Holy Spirit in the book suggests it could be called the Acts of the Holy Spirit. It is the story of Jesus doing and teaching through the Holy Spirit – using Peter, Paul and others.

The message of the book of Acts needs to be understood and applied. Acts is not a prescription of practices to be copied. It is a story, the story about what Christ taught through the agency of the Holy Spirit. We need to learn what He taught.

The first chapter sets the scene with the promise of the Holy Spirit to empower them to be witnesses to Christ. A witness is one who relates what he observed. This is the gospel of Christ – who He is, what He taught and what He did, in particular His death and resurrection. It is simple. It is not a whole lot of cultural forms enshrined into laws and regulations. It is the story of Christ.

Where were they to be witnesses? This introduces a major theme, if not *the* major theme of the book – the Holy Spirit would push them out of their comfort zone, Jerusalem and Judea, and into

Samaria and the ends of the earth.[39] Abraham's descendants were to be the source of the blessing of all peoples. With that ringing in their ears He left them.

The disciples had been instructed to wait for the promised outpouring of the Spirit. Meanwhile, they were still thinking in terms of Israel. They set their efforts to appointing a twelfth apostle. They believed that prophecy and their culture demanded a complete twelve in leadership. But the work of the Holy Spirit was about to begin in earnest.

The cultural message of Pentecost

The day of Pentecost came.[40] This was when the Jews celebrated the giving of the Law with all its details shaping the culture of the people. What an ideal day to re-educate them about His purpose, and to launch them into it! Not only that, at this time there were Jews from all over the regions round about gathered in Jerusalem. These Jews of the dispersion came with an understanding of the old covenant and the ability to listen to and speak many different Gentile languages. God chose this time as He wanted them to be part of the message He was announcing at this time.

The first thing they heard was the sound of a huge wind! They knew what that meant. Their word for 'wind' was the word for 'spirit'. Then came fire that divided into smaller tongues and settled above them. Fire was a symbol etched into their culture. They knew God used fire to designate where He was to manifest His presence. Moses had met it in the burning bush. The Israelites travelling through the desert were led by the fire and smoke. Directly where it stopped they knew this was where God wanted to manifest His presence. This was where they were to assemble the tabernacle

---

39. Acts 1:8
40. Acts 2

and place the Ark. Now in the upper room the disciples of Christ got the message. God wanted to manifest His presence, not in the temple up the road but in them. The believers in Christ were to be His holy temple – living, diverse and mobile, able to move to the distant parts of the earth.

Then came the first manifestation of His presence in them. They spoke the wonderful works of God. But they didn't speak in the traditional religious language that they all knew, Hebrew, the language in which they heard the Torah each Sabbath in the synagogue. Nor was it their commonly used local language, Aramaic. It was in Gentile languages – languages spoken by pagan people living in the ends of the earth. Was this Babel all over again? God was saying: "I want to diversify the way in which I manifest my presence. I want you to go into the world. I want all the diverse cultures of the earth to glorify Me!" Cultural diversity was indelibly etched into the initial manifestation of the infilling of the Holy Spirit.

As Steven explained to his accusers some time later, the whole earth and the people who live in it are to praise Him as His temple.[41]

The mono-cultural phase

With the newly given power of the Spirit, the apostles powerfully proclaimed the gospel in Jerusalem for about three years. But they didn't think to proclaim it to anyone other than Jews. Not only did they not know how to share the gospel cross-culturally, but they apparently didn't want to think through the implications of Jesus' plan for them! Finishing his speech to his accusers, Steven said: "You stiff-necked people... You are just like your fathers: You always resist the Holy Spirit!"[42] He would not have been thinking

41. Acts 7:44-50
42. Acts 7:51

that even his fellow believers still had something of this trait in them. They had not yet obeyed Jesus beyond Israel.

God nudged them again. This time He used a wave of persecution. Disciples were scattered to the countryside including Samaria. Samaritans were ethnically half Jewish. Jews avoided them because they were seen to make a hash of Jewish cultural forms. They didn't even see Jerusalem as the centre for worshiping God![43] Philip, not one of the apostles, had the courage to preach to Samaritans. Some responded to the gospel. Peter and John came to Samaria and laid hands on the new believers. Their faith was confirmed by them receiving the Holy Spirit. Philip shared the gospel with an Ethiopian. It seems that Philip was the first to catch on – the gospel was for Gentiles too! The scattering of believers continued to places where there were enclaves of Jews in Gentile towns and cities.[44] But initially, it seems, it was just to the Jews in these places that they related the good news. Meanwhile the apostles remained firmly located in Jerusalem and its surrounds. What would make them catch a vision beyond the borders – of 'the utmost parts of the Earth'?

The cross-cultural phase

The apostles still stuck to reaching and teaching Jews, until the Holy Spirit dramatically forced Peter to step into the next phase of the spread of the gospel.[45]

Cornelius was a Gentile Roman centurion. He was a God-fearer. He knew of and worshipped God but had not converted to Judaism. He was not a proselyte, and so he had not adopted Jewish cultural forms. Neither he nor Peter would seek each other out, but the Holy Spirit intervened to make them connect. He gave Cornelius a clear vision of an angel who told him to seek out Peter.

---

43. See the story related in John 4 about Jesus and the Samaritan woman.
44. Acts 11:19
45. Acts 10

Meanwhile, Peter probably thought he was having a nightmare in the middle of the day. It was lunch time. He felt hungry and started to get ready to eat. No doubt, he was about to do what all good Jews did, washing procedures in preparation to eat some kosher food. He fell into a trance and, horror of all horrors, he saw a bag of wild creepy crawly and flying animals descend before him, and a voice told him to kill them and eat them! Peter recoiled, "No way! I have never eaten anything common and unclean!" The voice replied, "What God has cleansed you must not call common." Whoa! After it happened the third time Peter was left wondering.

While he was wondering, the messenger from Cornelius arrived asking him to come to Cornelius' place in Caesarea. So the next day he went with them. When Cornelius gathered all his household together Peter explained what had happened to him and then reflected on God's impartiality and began to share the gospel of Jesus, and Christ's call for them to share it with 'the people'. Peter probably thought 'the people' were Jews or those who converted to Judaism. But to Peter's surprise, while he was still talking, the Holy Spirit fell on them and they began to magnify God in various languages. The Jews present were astonished. God had confirmed their faith – with Gentile languages. Gentiles who had adopted few or no Jewish cultural forms were included in the company of those who were cleansed by the blood of Jesus.

Back in Jerusalem Peter had some explaining to do! The Jewish believers said: "You went in to the house of uncircumcised and ate with them!" Peter told his story concluding, "…who was I to think that I could oppose God!" They too concluded, "Then God has granted even the Gentiles repentance unto life."[46]

Some believers from Cyprus and Cyrene began preaching to Hellenists (culturally Greeks) in Antioch. So the leaders in Jerusalem sent Barnabas (not one of themselves) to Antioch to encourage them

---

46. Acts 11:18

to continue with the Lord. It appears that the church in Antioch became the first church with a large proportion of Gentiles. It was in Antioch where Disciples of Christ were first called Christians.[47]

Against their inclinations, the Apostles found themselves preaching to, and welcoming into the fellowship of disciples of Christ, thousands of Gentiles. The book of Acts makes it very clear that this was purely on the initiative of the Holy Spirit. Cross-cultural evangelism and teaching was God's idea, not the Apostles'.[48] This opened up the potential of enormous numbers of followers of Christ. But the Spirit had to teach them yet more lessons before this could be realised.

Antioch was a large and influential and very much Gentile city. It was the Roman administrative centre for the whole of the east end of the Mediterranean. Culturally it was predominantly Greek, but there were other ethnic minorities living there, including a good number of Jews. The church grew under the leadership of an ethnically mixed group. It became the base for the apostolic journeys of Paul and his colleagues. Once again this endeavour began with the initiative of the Holy Spirit.[49]

The story of these journeys occupies much of the next eight chapters of the book of Acts. On the first journey, wherever they went they headed for the synagogue and shared the good news of Jesus in the cultural setting of the Jewish community. But more than Jews were listening. Gentiles were being impacted by the message and the powerful demonstration of the Spirit which confirmed their message. In Antioch of Pisidia we read that Gentiles begged to hear and almost the whole city turned out to listen. When opposed by the local Jews Paul told them, "We had to speak the word of God to you first. Since you reject it and do not consider yourselves

---

47. Acts 11:26
48. Chapter 7 The Hidden Message of 'Acts', in Richardson (1981) explains this well.
49. Acts 13:1-3

worthy of eternal life, we now turn to the Gentiles. For this is what the Lord has commanded us: 'I have made you a light for the Gentiles, that you may bring salvation to the ends of the earth.'" When the Gentiles heard this, they were glad and many believed.[50]

Thus we find Gentile believers increasingly being involved in the reception of the gospel, the sharing of the gospel, and the leadership of the fledgling churches. The scene was set for the Lord to jolt His church into the next huge mind shift.

The multicultural phase

The believers in Judea were living in a mono-cultural Jewish setting. They had had no reason to think other than the idea that all believers would accept Christ and in turning to Christ would convert to Judaism as a logical outworking of their repentance and new found belief system. Becoming Jewish proselytes seemed the only way to go. This would entail not only accepting a proper understanding of the nature and character of God and His moral demands on them, but also all the cultural forms of the Jewish faith. One of the first steps would be circumcision, the initial sign of becoming a member of God's covenant community. Then they should attend synagogue worship, keep food laws, and so the list would go on. This seemed neat and logical. It seems that an alternative to this did not enter their minds.

But news of what was happening at Antioch and further afield reached them. They heard that Gentile believers were not becoming proselytes. They were changing, but not adopting the Jewish cultural forms. They sent out messengers with the word that unless they were circumcised according to the custom of Moses they

---

50. Acts 13:44-48

would not be saved.[51] A big dispute was brewing. It was time to get together and work this issue through. Paul and Barnabas went up to Judea to meet with the Apostles and Elders in Jerusalem.

These church leaders came from different backgrounds. Some who were Pharisees said it was necessary to circumcise new Gentile believers and command them to keep all the Law of Moses. And so began the first major 'Church council'.

The first phase of the council was to let people have their say about this issue introduced by Paul and Barnabas. They had a spirited discussion. Then Peter, who now seems to be reconciled to God's multi-ethnic plan, began the summary process. He reminded them all that it was the Holy Spirit who included Gentiles in the faith. God made no distinction and purified their hearts by faith. So why should we argue with God and proceed to put on Gentiles a burden which we ourselves can't even bear. We all know it is by the grace of God (not our cultural forms) that we all are saved. Then they all listened again to Barnabas and Paul telling their story of the Spirit of God demonstrably confirming the reception of the gospel by Gentiles.

Finally James summed up. Firstly, he reminded them of what Peter had said. Then he quoted from Amos who prophesied about the judgment that the ancient kingdom of Israel would undergo.[52] The people would be sifted among the nations – sorting out the rubbish (the sinners) from the grain. Then God would restore the true Israel. God would raise up the tent of David. (Usually this is seen as a reference to the deposed dynasty of David, but possibly could be a reference to the tent which temporarily housed the glory of God, the Ark.) God's purpose was to repossess the Gentiles who would believe. The inclusion of Gentiles was in God's eternal plan.

Then he concluded that "we should not make it difficult for the

---

51. Acts 15
52. Amos 9:9-12

Gentiles who are turning to God".[53] They should not be required to adopt any Jewish cultural forms as a means to obtaining or enhancing their salvation. James recommended they write to the Gentile believers asking them to abstain from:

- things polluted by idols
- sexual immorality
- things strangled, and
- blood

The letter sent said it seemed good to them and the Holy Spirit to write to them about these decisions. It said, "If you do these things you do well." Later, when I look at what is written in the epistles about this issue, I will discuss what seems to be the reasoning behind these instructions.

Peter's reference to the purification of the hearts independent of their actions is reminiscent of Jesus' words about what makes a person pure – not what one eats but what is inside, which then is expressed by what comes out.

The significance of this decision is huge. The gospel could now be freely preached by Jews and Gentiles to Jews and Gentiles. The door was open to the multicultural spread of the gospel throughout the world. Had they decided to go along with the idea of believers becoming Jewish proselytes, they would have missed the whole nature of faith in Christ. Christianity would have lost its distinctive and would have been limited to being a subset of Jewish culture. The original multi-ethnic purpose of God would have been frustrated.

But they chose to go the multicultural way. The story in the book of Acts continues with the Holy Spirit pushing Paul, Silas and others further afield with the gospel. It was the Spirit's initiative

---

53. Acts 15:19

that moved them over the sea into Europe,[54] and on to the cultural centre of the empire, Athens, and then further toward Rome, the strategic governmental centre of the culturally diverse empire.

---

54. Acts 16:6-10

To study and discuss

1. Examine a map of the world. Identify where Jerusalem is.
- List the languages spoken on the day of Pentecost (Acts 2:8-12) and find their geographical source on a map of the Middle East and the Mediterranean.
- Find out where the influence of the Roman Empire extended.
- What places were at the ends of the Roman world?
- What places are at the end of the earth globally?

2. Peruse the book of Acts looking for references to the Holy Spirit.
- Make a list of what the Holy Spirit said and did.
- How many of these occasions are about pushing the apostles out of their comfort zone to fulfill chapter 1 v 8?

3. Visualize what would have happened if the church council in Jerusalem had decided all believers need to become Jewish proselytes.
- What would 'Christianity' have looked like?
- How wide spread would the faith be?

SEVEN

Cultural Freedom and Choices
in the Teaching of Paul

Paul had not been to Rome but he wanted to share with them the gospel as he had shared in other cities. Therefore, in the Epistle to the Romans Paul clearly spells out the gospel he preached. A unique feature of the gospel is that it is not about earning salvation through the effort of doing good deeds or conforming to cultural practices. It is about Christ. It is the power of God to bring about salvation, not by human effort, but by God's grace through faith in Him.[55] Paul is forcefully explicit about this. The first part of Romans spells this out clearly.

He says that Jews who ostensibly keep the Law and insist that others keep all the Law but in their hearts sin, make a mockery of the Law and bring shame on the name of God among the Gentiles. Circumcision is only profitable to those (Jews) who keep the Law in their hearts. Then the outward cultural forms are an authentic expression of what is in the heart. Gentiles who keep the Law in their hearts but outwardly are not circumcised show up Jewish hypocrites as sinners.[56]

He proceeds to explain how our righteousness does not come from doing the works (cultural forms) of the Law but from the work that Christ has already done.[57] Paul goes on to explain that

---

55. Romans 1:16
56. Romans 2:17-29
57. Romans 3,4

the believer's way of life is not one of being free to sin, but to be led by the Spirit and constrained by the love of God.[58]

Similarly in other epistles he moves on from what Christ has done to how we should continue to respond. In Ephesians he writes "I urge you to live a life worthy of the calling you have received."[59] In Philippians he writes "work out your salvation with fear and trembling".[60] Colossians has a similar progression of thought in it.

In Romans, like in each of these epistles, the latter chapters instruct on practical applications of this 'law of love'.[61] Firstly the emphasis is on attitudes of the heart – sincerity, brotherly love, honouring one another, diligence, and the like. Even payment of taxes and customs are expressions of fear and honour of God who ultimately ordained the civil government.[62] Any instruction to do a particular action is in the context of the heart attitude.

Cultural forms - 'scruples', but still to be scrupulously chosen

Clearly, for Paul, no action or cultural form has value in itself, positive or negative. He wrote, "I know and am convinced by the Lord Jesus that there is nothing unclean of itself."[63] Just like Jesus said, it is the inner source of the action, the attitude, the motivation that gives an action its value.

In Romans 14, he discusses disputes over 'scruples'. These include eating only vegetables versus eating anything, and esteeming one day of the week above others. To Paul, these are optional cultural forms. He wrote, "Let each be fully convinced in his own mind."[64] It is a personal choice, not an obligation. Whatever your

---

58. Romans 6-8
59. Ephesians 4:1
60. Philippians 2:12
61. Romans 12-15
62. Romans 13:1-7
63. Romans 14:14
64. Romans 14:5ff

choice is, it is to be done to the Lord. That is, it is to be an outworking of your heart of love for the Lord. We are each accountable to God, not to someone else who wants to impose an obligation on us.

It is interesting to note that, despite being one of the Ten Commandments, Sabbath keeping is regarded by Paul as an option for Gentile Christians. Clearly its position in the Law of Moses is not relevant. It would seem that, if it is a cultural form rather than a matter of the heart, it is not obligatory but chosen on the grounds of expediency.

The law of love motivates your choices

Paul goes on to examine your personal choice in the light of the 'law of love'. We all interpret one another by what we see them say or do. We have no other natural means to read each other. Our interpretation of each other's actions is coloured by our preconceived ideas about the person and by our cultural perceptions. Paul says your choice of action needs to consider how others will 'read' you.

So if your conscience is clear about your personal choice, you now need to consider the conscience of your brother or sister. Your choice may be interpreted by them as being more than a simple choice of action. They may see it has deep spiritual or attitudinal significance, and if he or she is one who looks up to you as a model or for spiritual guidance, you may lead him or her astray. If your choice should cause your brother or sister to stumble you should abstain from that choice, not because the action in itself is wrong, but because you love them.

Paul speaks of the one "whose faith is weak".[65] This may be one who is young in the Lord who needs guidance. On the other hand, he may be referring to one who has been a believer for some time

---

65. Romans 14:1

but who has not comprehended the fullness of the grace of God and puts transcendent value on certain good works. Often this will be a particular cultural form, such as keeping the Sabbath. Paul is clear. Don't criticise or argue with them. Instead, rejoice in their expression of the love of Christ whatever shape or form it takes rather than judging them on the basis of the cultural forms used.

Other Pauline epistles give similar teaching and instructions. In 1 Corinthians he applies the same principles to the issue of eating food which had been previously part of pagan idolatrous rituals.[66] Food is food and idols are powerless to us. The food we eat does not affect God's view of us. "Be careful, however, that the exercise of your freedom does not become a stumbling block to the weak".[67]

So the obligation was on those who were mature in the faith, those who knew they were free from the bondage of cultural forms, to accommodate the cultural perceptions of others. We adjust our cultural forms to edify those who read our actions through their cultural filter.

Most likely written about the time of the council in Jerusalem, the epistle to the Galatians is an aggressively emotional plea to the believers not to be pressured by Judaisers, Jewish believers, who insisted that Gentile believers should comply with Jewish law, starting with circumcision. Paul described those who were persuaded by them as 'foolish' and 'bewitched'.[68] The letter spells out similar teaching to that found in Romans about our justification in Christ and our subsequent freedom from the forms of the law. He also mentions an occasion where he perceived that Peter had not considered the gentile Christians when pressured by the presence of Judaisers.

Cultural forms "make a good impression outwardly"[69] – and

---

66. 1 Corinthians 8
67. 1 Corinthians 8:9
68. Galatians 3:1
69. Galatians 6:12-15

sometimes that is needed to connect to someone who is impressed by them – but it is the cross of Christ on the inside that impresses God. It is the cross that recreates you on the inside. Once again he summarises his plea with "in Christ Jesus, neither circumcision nor uncircumcision has any value. The only thing that counts is faith expressing itself through love."[70]

In the late 1980s and 90s, Michael Jones was a top NZ sportsman. He was a particularly rugged and consistent performer – a vital part of a very successful All Blacks rugby team. Yet whenever a match was scheduled for a Sunday he made himself unavailable to play. He made this choice to honour the Lord and his mother who was a devout Christian too. In the same team were other committed Christians who were his good friends, but chose to play on Sundays. They honoured each others' stand, and as a result of their attitude were an outstanding witness to Jesus Christ. They understood the teaching of the apostles in the New Testament. Their unity was in Christ, not the cultural forms with which they outworked their faith.

———

70. Galatians 5:6

To study and discuss

1. Revise this chapter and make a list of the contentious issues or 'scruples' Paul refers to.

- Now by referring to the chart in chapter one, which sets out a range of cultural forms, make a list of 'scruples' which Paul may have referred to had he been writing in our day.
- How is your attitude to those whose actions are different to yours on these issues?

2. In many cultures the excessive consumption of alcoholic drinks is very concerning. Consequently, drinking beer or wine has become a disputable issue in many Christian communities. Yet in others, particularly in societies where binge drinking is not a big problem, it is not a disputable issue! How do the principles taught in Romans 14 and 1 Corinthians 8 and 10 apply to this issue?

3. What are some other practices to which these scriptures are applicable?

EIGHT

The Importance of Cultural Forms

What James had to say

Paul emphasised salvation by the grace of God through faith in Christ. He repeatedly averred that no part of our justification is by human effort, by works. James on the other hand, writing in a similar time frame as when Paul was writing Galatians, stressed the need for believers' works to be seen. Some have tried to say the writings of Paul and James are contradictory. But those who say that have not understood James.

James says to be doers of the word not hearers only...[71] It is one thing to hear the gospel and it is another to really know it. Consistent with a truly Hebrew understanding of knowledge, James says to know Christ, to understand the gospel, to truly believe it, is to be committed to it. It involves doing it. Your faith is not complete unless it is worked out with corresponding actions. Paul agreed and expressed it this way: "…as you have always obeyed … work out your salvation with fear and trembling, for it is God who works in you to will and to act according to his good purpose."[72]

James had an understanding of the gospel the same as Paul. He called it the perfect law of liberty.[73] He did not deny we are justified

---

71. James 1:22
72. Philippians 2:12,13
73. James 1:25

by the grace of God through faith alone. We are set free from the bondage of doing good works to achieve salvation. He emphasised that the gospel demanded a response that could be seen. It demanded good works. Those works would be disciplined out-working of love in speech and action. He defied his readers to show their faith without doing good works.[74] He said that he himself showed others his faith by his good works.

He called these good works 'true religion'.[75] This is the only place in the New Testament where religion is spoken of as a positive attribute of believers. Elsewhere in the New Testament the word religion referred to the cultic and worship practices of Jews or Gentiles. The Latin origins of the English word religion help clarify its meaning. Connecting the words for 'of law', legis, and the verb 'to read', legere and the verb 'religare', which meant 'to place an obligation on', we get the gist of 'religion' being the reading again or repetition of binding rules.

If religion is binding oneself to cultic patterns of practice, the question to Christians is: "To what do you bind yourself and expect your brothers and sisters to bind themselves – Christ or specific patterns of practice or cultural forms?" If the answer is cultural forms your religion is a form of legalism. If the answer is Christ your religion is the Law of Christ. James says the true religion is…acts which stem from the love of God. You will work out your faith in Him by disciplined acts of love and purity.

What will these works look like? James does not define good works by set actions, but rather by describing attitudes such as impartiality rather than judgmentalism, loving your neighbour such as an orphan or widow, self control rather than unbridled speech, humility rather than lust, strife and boasting, and patience and perseverance with faith.

---

74. James 2:18
75. James 1:26,27

Thus we learn from James that patterns of practice which stem from our faith in Christ are important, even essential. The gospel is always expressed in a cultural form. But these acts have no value in themselves. It is the heart of faith in Christ that determines their value. It is the cultural context that determines their shape.

One way - many cultures

In his epistle the apostle John warns against loving the world. John describes "everything in the world" that we should not love as "the cravings of sinful man, the lust of his eyes, and the boasting of what he has and does."[76] These are not specific outward actions but attitudes of the heart which take expression in outward forms. For example, if clothing is the issue, it is not what you wear, but why you wear it that ultimately matters. It is not what style your clothes are that counts but what message about your heart they convey to others. Too often parents will target the cultural form instead of the attitude of heart when dealing with this issue.

For believers in Christ cultural forms take a different place in the schema of things. Our salvation is not dependent on the perform-ance of certain rituals or conforming to cultural forms. Other faiths are about achieving salvation through human effort, often involv-ing the obligation to adopt cultural forms. Islam, for example, can be described as the imposition of certain Arabic cultural forms.

A friend of mine was visiting a Hindu home in Fiji when a local Hindu holy man also visited. In the course of the conversation, the holy man said to my friend, "You would agree there are many ways to salvation." My friend said, "I kindly have to say, 'No'." Whereas Hindus believe in many ways of salvation but one culture – Indian culture, Christians believe there is one way, Jesus Christ, but many cultures in which the faith can be expressed. Hindus are usually

---

76. 1 John 2:16

comfortable with (or tolerate) many cultural forms, but the ones you inherit from your family must be adhered to, and they are seen as ways to salvation.

The role of cultural forms

Cultural forms are necessary. They play a vital role in the life of believers and non-believers.

Engaging. Cultural forms are a means of *connecting* with hearers. God worked with existing cultural forms to connect with the first Hebrews as he began to reveal Himself to these patriarchs of Israel. Likewise, evangelists can use a feature in the culture of their hearers to make connection in the communication of the gospel. Jesus used cultural forms in his parables to communicate truth about the Kingdom. Paul describes his personal choices as a matter of what is best for the promotion of the gospel.[77] To the Jews he became a Jew that he might win Jews. To the Gentiles he became a Gentile, to win Gentiles. To the 'weak' he became as one of them to win them.

This can be described as an 'incarnational' model. Because God loved the world, Christ became one of us to win us. Because we love the world we need to become one of them, at the level of cultural forms, to win them.

Educating. Cultural forms are a means of educating in the truth. God used the cultic (religious) practices He instituted in the Torah to educate the people of Israel about His holiness, the seriousness of their sin, the need of a saviour and the nature of that redemption. The book of Hebrews shows how the Mosaic Law foreshadowed and thus illustrated the more superior way in Christ. These cultural

---

77. 1 Corinthians 9:19-23

forms are an important means of educating us believers about salvation in Christ.

Cultural forms are necessary to teach children values. We teach children to be thankful by teaching them to say 'thank you', and by offering gifts or by other culturally acceptable means. These acts are all culturally determined. We do more than insist on the thankful action. We explain the reason why they should do this action, in the hope that they will learn gratitude and in time develop a habit of showing their gratitude by choosing appropriate culturally determined ways of expressing thanks. If we fail to help them make these connections there is a good chance they will just imbibe a cultural form. Yet instruction in the cultural form is a necessary part of the way we and our children learn.

Encouraging. Cultural forms shape our means of encouraging believers in the faith. Careful choice of practice, considering the cultural lens of those we wish to encourage, can help new Christians to work out their salvation, to grow in sanctification.

On the other hand, badly chosen practice can do the opposite. Your practice can be a 'stumbling block' to their progress in the faith. We make choices of our outward actions to edify our neighbour.[78] These choices will involve a consideration of the culture of those we will affect.

Expressing. Our faith is shown or outworked by cultural forms. As the book of James teaches, we show our faith by our works. For example, we must show love. The way in which we effectively do that will be determined by the motivation of love, the guidance of the Spirit, and the cultural context and perceptions of the recipient.

The motivation and ability to do good works does not come

---

78. Romans 15:2

from within your flesh but from God. True love stems from the heart of God and is focused on the recipient not on the fulfillment of one who shows that love. The actual shape of the actions will be determined by the cultural context and the prompting of the Spirit. Whether it is an act of charity, or a timely word of comfort or encouragement, its recipient must be able to receive it and inevitably that means it will have to be shaped by his or her cultural perceptions.

Specific cultural instructions in the epistles

We have seen that the clear teaching of the Apostles was that the gospel of Christ is about the transformation of the heart through faith in Him. We are saved by the grace of God, not by our effort. This grace demands our response. But that response is not defined by specific prescribed actions. An action's value is defined by the inward impetus, the source of the action – faith in Christ, the guidance and empowerment of the Spirit and by the love of Christ.

So how do we interpret the passages in the epistles where specific instructions are given? Let's take a simple example to start with. In Thessalonians we read, "Greet all the brothers with a holy kiss."[79] The inner intent of this instruction is that Paul wants the believers in the church to know that he as a close brother loves them. The way that this is to be communicated is by a "holy kiss". Why a kiss? The specific action is defined by the culture of the Thessalonians. If he had been writing to a group of Englishmen it would probably have been a 'hearty handshake', or to a New Zealand Maori group, a pressing of the noses, a 'hongi'.[80]

The cultural form with which we apply the teaching is determined not by the letter of the text but by the cultural setting in

---

79. 1 Thessalonians 5:26
80. The hongi has the concept of the sharing of breath, and can be an apt way of expressing unity of spirit.

which we are applying it. If we were to apply this by saying that we should greet one another by kissing, we are actually imposing first century Greek culture on ourselves. That is not the meaning of the New Testament. We would be imposing a new form of 'legalism'. We would be replacing the imposition of ancient Jewish cultural forms with the imposition of another set of cultural forms – and in some cultural contexts could convey a very confusing message.

Now let us apply this principle to 1 Corinthians 11 where Paul instructs the women to pray and prophesy with their heads covered and for the men not to cover their heads. The issue, it would seem, was contentious disrespect for authority – real or apparent. How you covered your head, or failed to, had meaning. Violating these cultural forms was signalling the wrong attitude. Modelling contention and disrespect even if your heart is right will not edify your neighbour. In verses 13 and 14, Paul appeals to them to judge for themselves as to what is proper behaviour, and to 'nature itself' teaching them. This appeal to what we would call common sense, and to what the natural mind would think, seems to be referring to the cultural sensitivities they have built in them. In a different cultural setting the same principles still hold. The attitudes must be right, but the cultural forms expressing them may be quite different. Once again, applying this instruction to cover or uncover the head in a 'legalistic' manner is imposing first century Greek culture on ourselves. The same principles apply when interpreting and applying other passages such as 1 Corinthians 14.

Recently I was visiting a reasonably insular community of believers whose cultural forms reflected the New Zealand of a few decades ago. My friend there asked me if a particular Christian school, that had shown them love when they were in need a few years ago, still had a woman as the principal (administrator). I said, "Yes, and she is currently the person to whom I am accountable in my work with Christian schools." This troubled my friend, who couldn't understand why a Christian organisation would have a woman in leadership. I let the matter drop from the conversation. I could have gone on to explain that my wife has been in leadership of Christian organisations for three decades. Sometimes I suggest to her that she respond to people who judgmentally question her leadership by explaining that she is in this position in deference to her husband and the call of God on our relationship and marriage. That usually ends the conversation!

What would have the apostle Paul thought about the increasing number of women in Christian leadership in many Western countries in the twenty-first century? In his letter to Timothy, he writes, "A woman should learn in quietness and full submission. I do not permit a woman to teach or have authority over a man, she must be silent."[81] He goes on to say that women can work out their salvation in the context of motherhood. We know that in the light of the clear New Testament teaching this advice was not given as a matter of law and righteousness but as a matter of expediency. We do not know the specific circumstances that existed in Ephesus where Timothy was, but we do know they lived in an incredibly patriarchal culture, where it was offensive for a woman to speak out in public without gaining permission from the men in authority. To do so would be seen as an act of outright insubordination. That cultural perception – how their action would be read in that culture – is enough reason for Paul to have that usual policy. Viewed from our twenty-first century Western context, this passage seems patriarchal. Viewed from the context of their ancient culture, it seems pragmatic or, as Paul expresses it, expedient.[82]

---

81. 1 Timothy 2:11,12. He then goes on to cite the order of creation (man before woman) and that Eve not Adam was deceived in the fall. We know that this is literally wrong – Adam was deceived as well. So it seems that Paul was using a hyperbole or could have been satirically paraphrasing Adam who blamed Eve for his sin. Whichever way, this is no grounds to interpret Paul's description of his normal policy as a universal principle, and so contradict his other clear teaching.
82. 1 Corinthians 6:12 and 10:23

The fact that he had to give instructions on this matter suggests that this cultural norm was somehow being questioned in the Ephesian church. They would have heard Paul (who lived with them for a few years) speak of the abolition of barriers, between Jews and Gentiles, slaves and freemen, and males and females, in Christ. They may have known some women with vocal roles in the church.[83] In attempting to outwork this in their community they may have 'pushed it' to the point of cultural offence.

There is a huge dilemma for an unmarried woman who has been given by God outstanding leadership abilities if she believes that the only legitimate way these gifts can be used is in the context of motherhood. I suspect that Paul would rejoice in the freedom to work out this issue freely in our twenty-first century Western culture – a freedom that does not exist in many places in the world and indeed did not in Western culture a generation or two ago. There are still many cultural settings in our current world, such as in the main meeting house (wharenui) on a New Zealand Maori marae, where it seems it is expedient for women to submit to the cultural norms.

Family responsibilities must be considered if you consider taking on a role that requires added commitment. In 1 Corinthians 7 Paul suggests that he recognised that his role as an itinerant leader in the church meant that marriage was not practical for him. In a culture where the role of women beyond the context of motherhood is encouraged, the practical reality of the high priority of the nurture of our children is to be seriously addressed by both mothers and fathers, but to confine Christian women to a subordinate role is another form of cultural legalism.[84]

Now, why did James and the council at Jerusalem make specific

---

83. E.g. Priscilla in Acts 18 and Romans 16:3, Philip's daughters in Acts 21:9, and Junias in Romans 16:7

84. 1 Corinthians 7: 32-35 discusses the challenge of choosing the expedient (not obligatory) path in the light of such priorities.

recommendations to the Gentile believers? Some have suggested that they were prescribing the Mosaic laws applicable to Gentiles. Others have connected these points of advice to the covenant made with Noah and his family (i.e. all of humanity) immediately after the flood. These factors may well be part of the mix, but James gave his reason for them – the existence of Jews in all the Gentile cities where they lived.[85] I suggest the council's and James' thinking was that these instructions were invoking God's universal moral law, in the case of abstaining from sexual immorality, and expediently avoiding cultural offense to Jews. Like any other believers, the Jewish believers in the city, being aware of the Law of Moses and not fully comprehending our freedom in Christ, could be caused to stumble by immoral or perceived immoral behaviour. As Paul also said, they should give no offense, either to the Jews or to the Greeks or to the church of God.[86]

These and other examples in the New Testament reinforce what James taught – that actions are important. It is in order for people in positions of authority to give specific instructions – in the home, in the church, the state or some other social setting. These instructions will not be transcendent laws but local rules stemming from what is expedient. The cultural setting will have its part in shaping what is expedient.

---

85. Acts 15:21
86. 1 Corinthians 10:32

To study and discuss

1. Peruse the book of James and make a list all the positive attitudes and character traits he advocates. Now next to each list two different ways in which it can be expressed.

2. A Christian parent is giving specific instructions to her young teenage child as to what clothes she may wear to an occasion outside the home.
- What Biblical principles must she consider?
- What specific rules could she enforce?
- If she were in another culture would the principles be the same?
- Would the specific instructions be the same?
- What teaching should accompany the specific instructions?

3. What should determine how specific a pastor or leader should be in giving instructions to their congregation?

NINE

Church Culture in the New Testament

The gospel of Jesus Christ penetrated into the Gentile world. Through its recipients, the believers in every city and town, it interacted with the local culture.

In the Roman Empire, the gospel interacted with the Greco-Roman culture in all its local variations. Each local church developed a pattern of practice as a result of the interaction of:

- the gospel of Christ as they understood it
- vestiges of ideas and habits brought into the Christian life from the old life, before conversion
- the ideas and cultural forms of the local community, and
- the influence of teaching and advice from without the community, such as the letters of Paul and others.

The resulting mix became the culture of the local church. The general pattern observed across the world eventually became known as 'Christianity'.

I have made a distinction between 'the Gospel' and 'Christianity'. I have defined Christianity as the result of the interaction of the gospel with the culture. There is one gospel of Christ, but different forms of Christianity such as Ethiopian or Syrian Christianity, or Eastern Christianity and Western Christianity as developed after the fall of the Roman Empire. And so, a local church can develop its own patterns of practice – its special brand of 'Christianity' while still proclaiming the same gospel as the church in the next town.

The patterns of practice were not always desirable. Paul wrote to the Corinthian church to correct their 'culture'. They had brought wrong attitudes and subsequent habits from their old life, which were affecting adversely the way they were relating to each other, and other cultural forms had to be examined in the light of their new relationships and understanding in Christ.

In the first two centuries it seems that the world did not consider the Christian faith as a 'religion'. It did not express itself as a set of practices to which followers conformed. It was seen as an alternative philosophy or as we say today a 'worldview'. Indeed it so lacked cultic practices of worship, early believers were accused of being 'atheists'.

Doing 'church'

The expressions (cultural forms) of early Christianity that did exist included patterns of meeting together. New Testament teaching made it clear they should not neglect gathering together to encourage and build each other up in the faith, telling the shared gospel story.[87] Paul instructed the Corinthian church about their meeting together saying "all things must be done for the strengthening of the church (the gathering)", and "everything should be done in a fitting and orderly way".[88] But the specific way in which this was to happen was a form to be worked out locally. What was 'fitting' was determined by what 'fitted' the need, the calling of God on the church, and the culture of the people the church was serving or reaching.

The first church in Jerusalem met as often as daily in homes as well as in the temple on the Sabbath. Some churches met on the first

87. Hebrews 10:25
88. 1 Corinthians 14:26-40 The specific instructions in this passage are addressed in the previous chapter.

day of the week. A regular river bank prayer meeting is mentioned. Meetings in a lecture hall are reported in Acts as well. Buildings specifically designed for Christian gatherings are not mentioned in the New Testament records. Initially there was no suggestion that a particular time and place was obligatory. That would have been the imposition of a cultural form, the antithesis of the gospel.

Baptism

When Paul arrived at Ephesus he met people who believed in Christ as a result of the work of Apollos. Paul asked them if they had received the Holy Spirit when they believed. They said, "No, we have not even heard that there is a Holy Spirit." So Paul asked, "Then what baptism did you receive?" "John's baptism," they replied. Paul proceeded to explain that John's baptism signified repentance but that baptism into Jesus Christ signified faith in Him. And so they were baptised into the name of the Lord Jesus.[89] It is interesting to note that the discussion was not about *how* they were baptised or the words used when they were baptised but the "*into* what" were they baptised – the understood significance of the baptism.

Public baptisms were part of the practice of early Christians. Baptism was a Jewish cultural form to which Jesus submitted Himself, and in the great commission He told His apostles to baptise their converts.[90] There is no biblical record specifying the details of how this should be done. The New Testament teaching speaks of the inner intent of baptism – a public declaration of faith in Christ and identification with Christ in His death, burial and resurrection, demonstrating a transformation of the conscience and a separation from the old life.[91] Once again how this is precisely done is not defined. This would be the imposition of a cultural form.

89. Acts 19
90. Matthew 28:19
91. e.g. Romans 6:3-11, Colossians 2:12

'Breaking bread'

Another pattern that was typical of the early church was to share a meal together. When Jesus shared His last Passover meal with His disciples he said, "…do this in remembrance of me."[92] It was clear that His followers needed to regularly celebrate His death in a way that educated and reminded them of the work He did for them on the cross. For Jewish Christians, the Passover meal or the Sabbath meal on the eve of each Sabbath was the time to do this. For Gentiles, they had to develop the best way to do this. A regular fellowship meal together was an apt cultural form to make a special effort to remember Him. Once again, they took this seriously, but the imposition of a specific cultural form would be antagonistic to the spirit of the gospel.

Giving

There is mention of giving honour to those who invest time in teaching the Word, and of encouragements to contribute to special collections of funds for specific projects. Giving was a significant practice, but there is no mention of tithing in the New Testament records of the early church. One reason for this could be that the local church leadership was not 'professional'. The local churches had neither staff nor buildings to maintain, but they did practice in a big way the care of widows and orphans. Many of the first church at Jerusalem sold property to share the proceeds. Tithing was a Jewish cultural form, and as such was not an appropriate obligation on the followers of Christ. Although we have no record of it being practised in Gentile churches it is possible some did tithe, but it was contrary to the gospel to impose such a cultural form on believers. Such obligation would be just another form of 'legalism'.

---

92. Luke 22:19, 1 Corinthians 11:24

Prayer

There was a culture of prayer. There are accounts of them praying together, and of a regular weekly prayer meeting, and in line with Jesus' teaching on prayer, it can be assumed the bulk of prayer happened in private. One church father commented that James prayed so much his knees were like those of a camel.

Most of their patterns of practice seen by the unbelieving world were clearly not religious cultural forms. The practices that were observed were mostly expressions of their care for and encouragement of one another, especially the organised and individual response to the needs of those in their fellowship who were poor or disadvantaged. Jesus had commanded them to love and followed it up with the comment, "By this all men will know that you are my disciples, if you love one another."[93] The apostles urged them to develop a culture of love.[94] The heathen world saw their 'true religion', their love and care for one another. This culture of love transcends all ethnicities, nationalities, social classes, genders or any other cultural sub-group. In each church there was the same love but it was expressed differently according to the local cultural context and circumstances.

Applying this flexibility of church culture, some modern successful church leaders say that they review everything they do as a church at least once every decade. No cultural forms, including Sunday services, are set in concrete. They are ready, if necessary, to completely reinvent all their church programs to fit the current need in the community and their calling as a church.

---

93. John 13:34
94. E.g. 1John 3:11

To study and discuss

1. Imagine you are a non-believer in your local community. Try and look at your church from their eyes.
- What do you think are the most notable things the world sees your church being or doing?
- Can the people of the surrounding culture read this and know what you are really on about?
- Is James' 'true religion' showing?

2. How is the culture of your church:
- faithful to the gospel, and
- appropriate for the culture of the community in which it is found?

TEN

Connecting with the Thinking of a Gentile Culture

One of the early dilemmas faced by the church was to work through the question of how much Christians should entertain the influence of the culture at large. What did Jesus mean when He prayed that they be in but not of the world?[95] This required careful thought and real discernment. At the external level, with cultural forms it was clear that New Testament writers were flexible. Forms which could truthfully express the truth of the inner work of Christ were welcome. But at the level of the inner world of ideas and values, there was no room for compromise.

A pagan culture had a mixture of ideas and values. Some would be compatible with the gospel. Others were anything but! The challenge was to discern which ideas could be utilised to connect people with the gospel and which were to be not entertained at all.

Paul in Athens

Luke records in the book of Acts key examples of sermons and proclamations to Jewish enquirers, to Jewish antagonists, to God fearers, and then to people of a completely different world view.[96] Paul's speech to the gathering at the Areopagus in Athens illustrates

---

95. John 17: 14-18
96. See Acts 2, 7, 10, 13 and 17

the use of the local culture to connect with the hearers. But he also corrects wrong ideas in the process of proclaiming Christ.

Paul did his homework and observed the culture and the thought patterns underlying the culture. He found a point of contact, "the Unknown God". He was careful not to choose a misleading one such as Zeus, the Greek god of gods but still an inferior part of the cosmos. He defined God properly and His relationship to the whole of the cosmos, both His eminence and His immanence. He explained God's impartial relationship to all humans. He was not just the God of the Jews. He explained how the worship of other gods or ultimate life goals are a result of ignorance or disobedience. He explained the need for all people to repent, and proclaimed Christ as ultimate Judge and Saviour, backing it up with the evidence of the resurrection.

John's Gospel

The introduction of the Gospel of John illustrates the use of Greek ideas to connect the readers with the story and identity of Christ. As idealists, Greek philosophers in general saw the real world as the world of ideas and the physical world as shadowy and transitory. The ancient Greeks, like many cultural groups around the world, recognised patterns and cycles in the order of the cosmos. They saw the universe as like a river and the order was upheld, sustained and controlled by the current or flow, the integrating essence of it all. They saw this essence or flow of the cosmos as more than an immaterial mindless influence. It was an intelligence or wisdom that was an integral part of the order of things. This 'soul' of the universe was called the Logos.

This wisdom of the cosmos was mysterious, yet was, at least in part, readable by intelligent beings such as ourselves. And so they attempted to read the universe by tracking its patterns and then attempting to align their life to it. They attempted to see the elements of earth, water, air and fire in various phenomena experienced in life. They developed a system of astrology to assist their quest to fit in with the patterns of the cosmos.

Their belief in their gods helped them explain the phenomena of the world which did not fit the perceived pattern. These gods were a mysterious part of the world, displaying human fickleness and weaknesses and so were part of the disruption of this ordered universe. But they would appease them with various sacrifices so their capriciousness would not be turned against them. In all of this they had no idea of the ultimate origin of it all. The gods were responsible for various phenomena in the cosmos, but how did the cosmos itself and the order and flow of it all get here in the first place?

Toward the end of what we call the first century, a man called John, living in this Greco-Roman world, wrote a biography with a difference – a strange postulation about a fellow Jewish man whose life he had witnessed over five decades earlier.

He began by writing:[97] *"In the beginning was the Logos."* Logos was the word used to describe the flow, the order, the wisdom of the cosmos. This the Greek readers would understand. John was claiming that the flow of the cosmos was also the original essence of the cosmos – a logical supposition.

"And the Logos was with God." Now this was a little radical. The term 'god' or 'gods' was used in relation to beings that had influence over events in the cosmos. But they were lesser beings *in* the cosmos, not beings pre-existing the cosmos, nor concurrent with the very order of it all. And the logos was with this personal being, before it all began!

"…and the logos was God." Now this is hard to comprehend! How could the logos be with God and be God at the same time? Clearly, for this to be true, categories and qualities of the phenomena of this

---

97. John chapter 1

world do not fit. John's logic means the logos/god is out of this world! Yet this concept explains the mysterious intelligence of the order or flow of the cosmos. The logos is more than mindless influence. The logos has personhood. The logos is a person in the act of revealing himself or speaking. The logos is the pre-existent, non-corporeal God speaking, revealing himself. The logos is "the word of God".

"He was with God in the beginning." John reiterates that the logos is not part of the cosmos which had a beginning in time, but pre-existing the cosmos. Yet the logos is in and through every aspect of the cosmos. He is the very essence of the flow of the cosmos.

"Through him all things were made." The logos is not only the sustaining power of the cosmos, but the creative power of God to make it all in the first place.

"Without him, nothing was made that has been made." Not only was the logos the initial creator, but the ongoing creator of everything since. Everything we or any other creation creates is in essence him creating it through us! Yes, the ongoing creative force of the cosmos is the original creator. Nothing is self-sufficient. To continue to exist, all is dependent on the logos.

"In Him was life and that life was the light of all people." The life force sustaining us all and causing us to live, to move, to reproduce and to influence our environment is the logos/God. This life force is also the source of all enlightenment, all knowledge. The life force is the intelligent creator and sustainer of everything.

With further words John continues to relate and explain a story about the logos being in the world but not recognised by the world.

And then he writes: *"The logos became flesh and made his dwelling among us."* Now this is not only hard to comprehend, but totally mind-boggling! The eternal flow of the universe becomes a person!? John claims that this person was Jesus of Nazareth. Jesus is the anointed One, the logos, the life force, the flow of the whole universe encapsulated in a single person!

And so John wrote his story of the life, death and resurrection of Jesus Christ, each aspect backing up his claims about his identity.

"...These are written that you may believe that Jesus is the Christ (the anointed One), the Son (very essence) of God, and that by believing you may have life in his name."

The message of the gospel of John is to proclaim the identity of Jesus, so that the readers might trust in him, and thus receive that eternal life force. John urges readers to commit their lives to Jesus Christ since he is the creator, sustainer, the flow, the life force of the universe.

These are often referred to examples of the apostles using the culture in which their hearers lived to make connection with them. Clearly both Paul and John had more than just a superficial understanding of the Greek culture. They had a deep understanding of their thought patterns. Without compromising the truth, they used that understanding to communicate the good news of Jesus.

To study and discuss

1. Find information about the Muslim understanding of God.
- If an evangelist was introducing God to some Muslims, like Paul was connecting the Athenians to God, do you think he/she could use their idea of Allah as a point of connection to God?
- What aspects of the idea of Allah would truthfully convey what God is like?
- What characteristics of Allah would be totally misleading?

2. How would you communicate the identity of Jesus to:
- a Buddhist or
- a person of 'new age' persuasion?

CULTURE IN CHURCH HISTORY

ELEVEN

Christianity in the Roman Empire and Middle Ages

Being salt and light

The challenge for the emerging church was to engage the culture of the world without being engulfed by the thought patterns of the world. Jesus taught that believers were to be salt and light.[98]

The main purpose of salt was to intensify the taste of and preserve food by being mixed through it. The followers of Christ were to mix in the world and so transform and preserve the culture of the people in which they were placed. But Jesus warned that the danger would be that, like salt mixed too thinly can lose its saltiness and hence its ability to be effective, believers can lose the essential distinctiveness of their faith by absorbing the wrong thought patterns from the worldly culture around them.

The purpose of light is to enable us to see the world for what it is and make our way through it effectively. Thus Jesus was saying that believers were to proclaim the truth in word and deed so that others would see the truth. To do this effectively it is necessary to stand out from the crowd. The danger is that in being separate from the world we can become isolated and hence invisible like a lamp under a bowl, and have no real effect on the culture of the people in which we live. We must stand out visibly, in all the visible dimensions of cultural life.

---

98. Matthew 5:13-15

This means our transformed inner life will impact and transform our outer life, in the realm of cultural forms. It is when we are seen doing things differently, not in a culturally offensive way but in a way that is culturally acceptable and even appealing, that we will make a difference in the world. When we are seen to show compassion, impartiality, self control – the very things James spoke about – in a way that is not culturally offensive, people are drawn to us and thus to Christ.

Jesus said you plural are the salt of the earth and you plural are the light of the world. He was referring to His followers corporately. He was teaching that relating to the world was not to be just an individual thing, but also to become a pattern of practice characteristic of all the church.

The dangers that Jesus mentioned related to being salt and light are often not manifest as much in the first generation of believers, as in the next or ensuing generations. Children of believers easily absorb the cultural forms of their parents' generation but can resist the transformation of the heart that comes with the gospel. They become what we may term 'cultural Christians'. They can practise the cultural forms of being a Christian – speak in Christian talk, go to church, even be baptised take communion and pay tithes, but fail to relate to the Lord in the heart. How can this be avoided or at least minimised? This is a question that Christian history can help answer. This process of falling away is repeated over in Christian history, and is contrasted by generations who did not.

Many early church fathers chose not to read or entertain the thoughts of classical Greek authors. The problem of being tainted by the wrong thoughts of Gentile thinkers was a reality right from the beginning. Parts of the epistles now found in scripture were written to counter the emergence of Greek ideas in the first generation of believers. It was too great a risk to be tainted by the world, so rather than interacting with and confronting the wrong ideas of the world, some isolated their minds from the world.

On the other hand some chose to take a different approach. Some suggested that the Greek philosophers asked the right questions and Christ had the right answers. They argued along the lines that unless we grapple with the ideas of the world and throw the light of God's revelation on them we will not influence the thought patterns of the world. But the danger is imbibing the ideas of the world and beginning to give them as much authority as we do to God's Word. Then it is easy to deny the authority of the Word in certain areas of life, and eventually to deny its authority in any.

On the whole it would seem that the first generations of believers were ostracised from the general population and kept the inner life of the faith comparatively pure. But in the fourth century as the faith became more accepted, the danger of the church losing its saltiness became an increasing reality.

The entrenchment of cultural forms

The legalising of Christianity in AD313 allowed Christian cultural forms to be practised in public without fear of penalty. But it also meant that people whose hearts were not committed to the Lord would be free to practise them too. That in itself was not a problem, but it fudged the observable differences between those whose hearts were committed to the Lord and those who maybe were not. Now inheriting your parents' Christian cultural forms without being transformed within by the gospel became a real possibility.

Then, a generation or so later, when in AD381 Christianity became the official state religion of the Empire; cultural Christianity was not only possible but legally enforceable. The state's function was making laws and regulations. The state could not observe the heart. The state could only act on observable words and actions. The state could impose cultural forms, but not change the heart. Standard Christianity could become another form of 'legalism' – state enforced religion.

It appears that with the marriage of church and state, Christianity began to lose its heart. With each succeeding generation Christianity became more a matter of cultural forms than a living relationship with Christ. With the focus on cultural conformity came a loss of an understanding of the cross-cultural mission. Attending church on Sunday morning became the legally required form of behaviour. Dressing up on Sunday became important as you may be observed by the Emperor or someone important at church. Ecclesiastical structures and rituals began to assume the centre stage instead of the gospel of Christ which these forms were meant to manifest and serve.

When the cultural forms became disconnected from the gospel, they became distorted and added to by non-Christian influences. There was less ability to discern between cultural forms that were an outworking of the gospel and those that were pagan tradition. They were all regarded as part of Christianity.

Referring to the 'middle ages', Francis Schaeffer[99] described it this way:

> ...the pristine Christianity set forth in the New Testament gradually became distorted. A humanistic element was added: Increasingly, the authority of the church took precedence over the teaching of the Bible. And there was an ever-growing emphasis on salvation as resting on man's meriting the merit of Christ, instead of on Christ's work alone. ... Much of Christianity up until the sixteenth century was either reaction against or reaffirmation of these distortions of the original Christian teaching.
>
> These distortions generated cultural elements which mark a

---

99. Schaeffer (1976, p. 35)

clear alternative to what we could otherwise call a Christian or biblical culture. …It would be a mistake to suppose that the overall structure of thought life was not Christian. Yet it would be equally mistaken to deny that into this structure were fitted alien or half-alien features – some of Greek and Roman origin, others of local pagan ancestry – which at times actually *obscured the outlines of the Christianity underneath.*

When Charlemagne, the Frankish king, was crowned emperor by the pope in AD800, the church and state became co-influential. Through the state the church had huge power to enforce Christian cultural forms. Tithing, for example, became compulsory. State funds were channelled into church administration and church buildings and were used to found a Christian singing school and foster Christian scholarship. Thus Christianity became a mix of scholarly thought and enforced cultural forms. Such was the shape of Christianity in the Holy Roman Empire.

Monastic culture

The monastic movement rose during these times. The desire to foster a right relationship with God rather than be influenced by the tainting of the world was strong. Monasteries were often the sole centres of genuine faith, learning and Christian service in a community. Orders such as the Benedictines and Dominicans formed enclaves of faithful monks through Europe. Their founders established effective rules of conduct which helped them in their relationship with God and service to the world.

Benedict in particular is remembered for his 'Rule' for the monastic life. Written in the early sixth century, Benedict's 'Rule' was obeyed or commended by many to follow. It was made the official rule for all monks in Charlemagne's empire. Moderate in its provisions, it served well many entering the monastic life. Central to the "Rule" was obedience – to Christ, the Rule and the abbot. This was its strength and ultimate weakness. Sadly, the same trends unfolded. Reminiscent of the detailed rules of the Jews added to the Torah, the rules too often became patterns of practice passed on to and imposed on future generations of monks.

Although the detailed records are not as plentiful, it would seem that in some other parts of the world also Christianity lapsed mainly into the passing on of cultural forms.

In the early Middle Ages, Christianity not only endured in Europe, it grew. There were pockets of genuine vibrant faith in Christ and His work on the cross, of active evangelism, and resulting cultural transformation. This was particularly so in the monastic movement and on the geographical or cultural fringes of what was becoming known as Christendom.

Life on the fringes

Beginning with Patrick in the fifth century in Ireland a movement sprang up in Celtic north-west Europe that lasted for at least two centuries. Patrick came from Britain not Ireland. He was a slave in Ireland in his youth. He trained in a community in what is now France before responding to the call of God to return to Ireland to share his faith. It is common knowledge that his work was amazingly successful. The gospel transformed the lives of many and then was applied to the whole of the culture. The result of the interaction of the gospel with existing Irish culture was lasting. Evangelists and teachers trained in schools for monks and took the gospel to the Celtic world. The most remembered school was the Abbey established by Columba on the island of Iona in Scotland.

This movement was not part of the mainstream Roman based church. St Bede, in his history of the British church, commends the life of many of these heroes of the faith, but found disagreement with them on certain points such as they celebrated Christmas on the wrong date. This reflects the commitment to standard patterns of practice by the seventh century Roman based church, of which Bede was part, and the Celtic Christian movement's independence when it came to cultural forms. When Augustine came to England to inculcate the British believers in the practices of the Roman church, he found it necessary to confront these Celtic monks with a whole range of Roman practices which differed from the local practice. It took two generations of interaction to arrive at a degree of agreement on cultural forms.

The success of the Celtic Christian movement can be put down to various factors among which are:

- their commitment to Christ and the foundational truths of the gospel,
- their application of it to the whole of their culture, and
- their ongoing involvement in cross-cultural evangelism and teaching in the Celtic world.

The first of these may seem self-evident. A Christianity without Christ has nothing to maintain to call Christian. Latourette[100] examined all the branches of Christianity including those that have been generally classified as heretical, and reflected that those movements which had the most lasting effect were those that most clearly maintained the centrality of and ultimate significance of Christ.

The second is important. A faith which does not impact the whole of life becomes considered irrelevant and will be consigned to history. The Christian faith of one generation is passed on to the next through education using cultural forms connected to the truth of the inner life of the believer. The cultural forms alone lead

---

100. Latourette, (1937)

to formal cultural Christianity, but the unapplied faith is no faith at all, as James insisted.

The third is often overlooked. Patrick did not impose Roman cultural forms on the Irish Celts he evangelised. The Irish connected to the gospel that Patrick and his colleagues preached because it was presented in Irish terms and looked Irish in its manifestations. To then communicate this faith in a truly cross-cultural manner, applying it to a new culture required an understanding of the faith – the core theology of the gospel – as distinct from the cultural expressions of it. Cross-cultural evangelism and teaching of the faith is an effective factor in ensuring that the faith does not lapse into formalism or legalism.

To study and discuss

1. Choose two movements (sects or para-church ministries) which emphasise either being light or being salt. For each identify the advantages of this emphasis and the dangers (even errors) resulting from this emphasis.

2. Review the section in this chapter on the entrenchment of cultural forms. Then have a debate on the topic: You cannot legislate morality.

3. What cultural forms became the centre of Christianity in medieval times?

4. Research a little about the monastic movement.
- What was good about the monastic movement?
- How did it line up with James' 'true religion'?
- What inventions can be attributed to the monks in the middle ages?

5. Research the lives of some Celtic Christians such as Patrick, Columba, Brendan, or Aidan. How are they great examples for us to emulate?

TWELVE

The Power and Vulnerability of the Kingdom

The world abounds with cultures that have been radically changed by the influence of Christianity. Not the least of these is the general culture we call 'western'. Although full of imperfections, Western civilisation with its freedoms, care for human life and rights, democratic principles and scientific and technological advances is a story of the triumph of a culture shaped by a biblical Christian world view engaging the culture of the people.

Yet the story of the spread of Christianity has not been a consistent steady expansion. In some locations it appears to have retreated. In places where the faith was initially centred, such as the east end of the Mediterranean and north coast of Africa, the Christian faith has mostly been superseded by Islam.

Why does Christianity appear to be so powerful and yet so vulnerable to decay? The answer lies in the nature of the Kingdom of God.

The inside out kingdom

As described by the gospels, Jesus came preaching the gospel of the kingdom. He taught that the kingdom of God/heaven was His kingdom and that His kingdom was not of this world. He described it as God's will being done on earth as it is in heaven. He taught that unless we are born from above we won't see, let alone enter, the Kingdom. He taught that it was near. He taught us to seek His kingdom. The Sermon on the Mount begins with keys to the blessing of the kingdom being certain attitudes. He taught that the Kingdom was within. He illustrated His teaching with parables – the kingdom is like a good crop mixed among weeds, like yeast mixed in flour, like treasure found in a field, like a net of good and undesirable fish, like a mustard seed that grows into a dominant tree in the garden. He taught that there were expressions of the kingdom such as acts of compassion and power.

The foundations of the rule of God, Christ's Kingdom, are matters of the inner person. The kingdom is not identical with the outward manifestations of the kingdom. Jesus warned of those who would cast out demons in His name and would not enter the Kingdom. The church is not the Kingdom. The church was called by Christ to be the prime agent of the Kingdom. A Christian civil government is not the Kingdom.[101] Men and women transformed by the gospel and working out that transformation through deep involvement in the processes of government are an expression of the Kingdom.

The Kingdom begins not with a military or political victory, but with the gospel winning the hearts of repentant individuals. The power of the Kingdom is the power of the gospel of Christ and of the work of the Spirit of Christ. It begins on the inside of humans and then works out into observable actions in families, communities, and nations. It begins with legions of principalities and powers, the wrong ideas and attitudes that have captivated

---

101. In recent decades the Western world has virtually made democracy an ultimate virtue. Democracy is a cultural form that has arisen out of the cultural foundation of a biblical understanding of what it means to be human, but it is not the foundation in itself. The last 50 years have seen the imposing of democracy on nations where it has on the whole not worked, not because democracy is wrong but because the cultural foundations of democracy (wisdom and virtue arising out of a biblical world view) have not been present in a sufficient proportion of the population.

the hearts and minds of people, being cast out. It begins with the Spirit of Christ coming in. Then the signs of the Kingdom, transformed lives expressed in transformed relationships, compassion and dreams being miraculously worked out in social and political action, become seen.

The style of Kingdom leadership is radically different in God's Kingdom. In the world's kingdoms it reeks of control. The leader lords it over the others – it is about position and prestige. The leadership in the kingdom of Christ is characterised by sacrificial service.[102] It is commonly referred to as 'servant leadership'. Servant leadership is not servitude, but rather inspiring, encouraging and facilitating others to excel in their gifts. It is practising 'the cross of Christ'.[103] This is one of many aspects of the Kingdom of Christ which is counter-cultural. Paul Trebilco puts it this way:

> At heart then, there is a fundamental contradiction, even opposition, between the Gospel and the world… For it goes against the grain, and operates from a different wisdom."[104]

The growth of the Kingdom depends on the growth of the rule of Christ in people's hearts, not on the compulsory passing on of cultural forms from one generation to the next. As sinners we resist the rule of Christ in our hearts. The 'natural man' is wired to be attached to the cultural forms he experiences in his formative years and then to protect and conserve them. Herein lies the source of the wide scope of transformative strength of the gospel and at the same time the apparent weakness of Christianity to persist throughout generations.

Because the gospel of the kingdom is about the heart, it has no

---

102. Matthew 20: 20-28
103. Philippians 2:1-11
104. Trebilco, (2006) in Carson (2008, p. 171)

cultural bounds. It can penetrate any people group. The rule of Christ is thus revolutionary. It can change the people from within and then engage with the culture of the people. It can then transform the culture. It can change the world, while the world remains culturally diverse. In this way the ultimate future fulfilment of the Kingdom can be culturally diverse.

Handing down the keys of the kingdom?

Jesus quizzed His disciples about their understanding of His identity. It was Peter who answered, "You are the Messiah, the Son of the Living God." Jesus pointed out to him that this was a revelation directly from God the Father. Peter was the first to confess this revelation. On the basis of this rock He would build His church – His worldwide body of believers, and He would give them the 'keys of the Kingdom' – the ability to operate in the realm of the Spirit.[105]

God does not have grandchildren. Each generation needs to repent, to be changed by the gospel, and have their inner lives transformed by the power of the Spirit. As Jesus pointed out to Peter, they can't inherit the revelation – they must receive it themselves directly from God the Father. Then they can get the keys of the Kingdom, not from their parents but from the Lord. So what can happen to the children of those who have the keys of the Kingdom – the next generation?

They can observe and learn the culture in the process of transformation. They can also be taught the reasons for this culture – the heart of the culture. They can be pointed to Christ and can be fervently prayed for. But it is up to them to respond to the call of the Spirit and open their hearts to the transforming power of the gospel and then allow the Lord to use them to continue the transformation of the culture.

---

105. Matthew 16:13-20

But what if they imbibe the culture of their parents' generation but do not engage their hearts with the King of the Kingdom culture? Their Christianity becomes a pattern of practices, a series of cultural forms, by following which they believe they are Christians. They become what we may term 'cultural Christians'. As expressed in the beginning of the previous chapter, they can practise the cultural forms of being a Christian – speak in Christian talk, go to church, even be baptised take communion and pay tithes, but fail to relate to the Lord in the heart. These signs of the Kingdom become false signs because the heart of the Kingdom and the King are not present. In one generation the heart of the faith is lost. This state of mere 'cultural Christianity' can continue for a few or many generations. It is quite possible the next generation may not even be taught who God is and what He has done. And even as soon as the third generation the culture shows signs of collapsing.

The culture with its Christian forms progressively loses its rationale. It is vulnerable to attack. Not only can the foundational relationship with Christ be absent but the foundational presuppositions of the faith will begin to fall away. It will sooner or later fall prey to the invasion of other ideas and other values. With the centre of the culture, the good news of Jesus removed, the culture will change shape and sooner or later collapse.

Walls expresses it this way:[106]

Christian history reveals the faith often withering in its heartlands, in its centers of seeming strength and importance, to establish itself on or beyond its margins. It has vulnerability, a certain fragility, at its heart – the vulnerability of the cross, the fragility of the earthen vessel.

On the other hand, a new kingdom movement can begin within

---

106. Walls (2002, p. 67)

the people of the culture. A revival, renewal or reformation can take place. Hearts can once more be transformed and the Christian practices in the culture can once again be reinforced.

The invasion of worldly kingdoms

In the Middle Ages around the eastern and southern shores of the Mediterranean, a new set of ideas invaded and captured the minds of the people. This pattern of ideas and accompanying cultural forms was Islam. Islam was a kingdom movement. Unlike the gospel of Christ, it was a kingdom of this world. It came by military or political persuasion. Allah could never be a sacrificial servant. It came with a pattern of practices, a set of cultural forms which constituted holiness. It enforced submission to this 'rule of Allah', Islamic law. The heart of Islam was submission to the law of Allah. It was forcefully compelled upon generation after generation and so usually did not geographically retreat. As a compulsory culture, the kingdom of Islam was not subject to the same vulnerability as the Kingdom of Christ.

Meanwhile in Western Europe, at various times and in various places, there were pockets of renewal. Christianity held its ground. But when the pervading form of Christianity was merely cultural, it was vulnerable to the attack of other ideas. Christendom maintained a degree of political and cultural isolation from the rest of the world. It was not taken over by a complete new set of ideas and cultural forms, but it morphed into a perpetuation of traditions within the framework of a Christian world view, albeit a set of half truths. It was called Christendom because it had become a territorial kingdom of this world with political power and the enforcement of cultural forms. The crusades were a manifestation of a worldly kingdom. Christendom was ripe for the invasion of alien ideas – or the rediscovery of the truth.

To study and discuss

1. Read a series of Jesus' parables of the Kingdom. How does each one contribute to the concepts of what the Kingdom is like?

2. Under the headings:
- The true Kingdom of God,
- Medieval Christendom, and
- Islam

list their contrasting or comparative features.

3. Make a list of cultural forms that you think characterised 'Christendom'.

THIRTEEN

Reforming the Culture

Toward the end of the Middle Ages Christendom did become influenced by ideas from without. They were basically the ideas, the cultural foundations of Greek culture – the ideas the early church had interacted with and grappled with a millennium before. The thinking of the great Dominican scholar of the thirteenth century, Thomas Aquinas, opened up Christendom to new ideas.

Truth had become the domain of the church hierarchy. It was all about the unseen universals which gave morals and existence meaning. This was reflected in the art of the time which depicted heavenly beings and saints rather than ordinary things of creation. The reading of Greek philosophers such as Aristotle was forbidden in the universities of the thirteenth century. Aquinas rightly valued the particulars of creation as well as the universals. But he taught an incomplete view of the fall – that the mind was not fallen. This opened up the thinkers in Christendom to adopt the ideas of Greek thinkers like Aristotle, and these ideas gained equal credence alongside the Bible in the thinking of the church.

Now this led to two paths of thought to follow. One was to pursue ideas stemming from examining or observing the particulars of creation. This was the path of the pioneers of what would become modern science. The other was to reject this renewed interest in particulars of creation and reaffirm the authority of the church as the sole source of truth. Hence there arose conflict between the established church and men such as Galileo.

The culture of the Reformation

This return to the founders of thought also started a move to re-examine the original texts of scripture and its original application. The core of the gospel as recorded in the New Testament – that we are made right with God through faith in the work of Christ – was rediscovered. Europe experienced the Protestant and subsequent Catholic reformations. The biblical approach to understanding creation particulars in the light of spiritual universals had opportunity to emerge. Many people's hearts were turned to faith in Christ. The art of the time, for example, began to feature ordinary people and ordinary things as reflections of the glory of God. The authority of the church was questioned and cultural forms were released from the dictates of the church hierarchy. Creation was examined by the early scientists and was seen to exhibit the mind and the glory of God.

At the centre of the Protestant reformation was the rediscovery of the heart of the gospel, salvation by the grace of God through faith in the finished work of Christ. If salvation was through faith alone, and not through devotions involving statues, carvings, stained glass windows and frescoes, the value of these objects was questioned. In the middle of the 1530s there was an orgy of image breaking. Some of Europe's best art works were destroyed. This iconoclasm (or vandalism) was misplaced. The problem was not these works of art but the use of them as an alternative means of salvation and as objects of worship. The church hierarchy's defence was that these art works, created as an expression of faith and devotion to the Lord, were not objects of worship but aids to worship. They argued that if we abandon our respect for the cultural forms of religion we could easily come to reject the core values and beliefs. The reformers said that the church had already abandoned the core values and beliefs and had substituted these idols.

The Protestants needed some other means of expressing their thanks to the Lord, their joy of being justified by the grace of God, and their devotion to the Lord. A major way of expressing their faith was through singing. In an age before recordings, singing left no objects to be misused as objects of worship. It could not be a target for destruction like icons were. But the reality was that, as a cultural form, singing could become more than a way of expressing worship and could usurp the centre stage, becoming the focus of worship.

Some years ago I was travelling by public transport between cities in Australia. I sat next to a young woman who was travelling to an Easter youth camp run by a particular denominational group. She belonged to a church in a different stream but suggested she might change because 'their music was better'. Thus began an interesting conversation about what was the object of her worship and church attendance. As essential as it is to have them, we must never let our patterns of practice (cultural forms) become the centre of our Christian culture. Christ is the centre and our cultural forms should surround and exalt Him.

Since the reformation, as usual, each generation has tended to drift away from the heart of the gospel and revert to only perpetuating traditions, patterns of practice, cultural forms. Each generation needed to engage the gospel themselves.

Subsequent reformation of culture

During the last four hundred years there have been at various times and in various places special times of engagement with the gospel of Christ. We have called them renewals, awakenings, revivals or reformations. They have been vital in keeping the church of Christ in touch with Christ. It is out of these that have come various cultural reforms. The Great Awakening and the Wesleyan revival of the eighteenth century led to the reformers of the next generations. These reforms included massive cultural changes such as the abolition of slavery on the basis of race, the education of the masses stemming out of the Sunday school movement, the development of the modern nursing profession, the abolition of child labour, the care of prisoners, exploited workers and the disadvantaged in society. The revivals of the mid-nineteenth century in America stemmed a tide of violence and family breakdown.

Some patterns of practice reflecting the heart of Christ were established and affected not just the redeemed but the general population. The gospel of Christ caused cultural change. Sadly, many Christians resisted the change of renewal, often forcing those caught up in the renewal to 'break away'. Often they resisted change because established patterns of practice, which they considered essential to their faith, were threatened or challenged. Many of the various main stream protestant denominations arose over differences on such things as patterns of church government or of forms of baptism. An appreciation of the unity of spirit we have and of the non-essential nature of cultural forms must be a key factor in fostering unity.

To study and discuss

1. Investigate the life of a famous musician, artist or scientist whose life was committed to Christ and who became a leader in his field e.g. Bach, Handel, Newton or Faraday to name a few – in what way did his faith affect his practice?

2. Discuss the role of cultural forms such as music, rituals or festivals in your church.
- Are they the focus or do they help people focus on Christ?
- How could they better direct people's attention to Him?

3. It has been said that sects (denominations) vary on patterns of practice while false cults vary from the rest on the core of the gospel.
- What are the chief variations between the main Christian denominations?
- Do they match up with the above idea?

FOURTEEN

Culture and the Modern Missionary Movement

At the same time as this cultural reformation was happening in Europe and America, exploration opened up a fresh awareness of the world beyond Christendom.

Emigration from Europe to establish colonies based on a Christian view of society became a reality. The Spanish 'invaded' Central and South America and other places they had discovered, bringing with them the cultural forms of Spanish Catholicism. Despite the efforts of many faithful priests, the Spanish came on the whole with the methods of the kingdoms of this world – become a baptised Christian or else become slaves or immediate history.[107] Because the real gospel, the cultural foundation of Christianity, was on the whole not established, the fruits of economic, political and social prosperity were very tenuous.

On the other hand a significant number of immigrants to North America came with the gospel of inner transformation through faith in the grace of God. Thus biblical cultural foundations were laid in the hearts of many of the settlers. The Puritans especially came also with an expectation of working these foundations out into all aspects of life. The ensuing result was a comparatively better measure of economic, political and social prosperity.

---

107. This methodology and that of the Spanish inquisition could well have been a vestige of the influence of the Moors (Spanish Muslims) on Spanish culture.

The Book of Acts revisited

Renewals of faith in Europe and America stirred in the conscience of believers a fresh understanding of God's heart for the masses of people outside of the 'Christian' West. The amazing story of the missionary movement of the last two centuries parallels the book of Acts in many ways.

Christian Europe and America had become like the Jews of old, having a European mono-cultural vision. They had lost the cross-cultural vision that God had in the very beginning and that the first generation of apostles learnt from the Holy Spirit. Christendom was very inward looking. The pioneers of the missionary movement such as William Carey had to work extremely hard just to convince the church that they needed to take the good news of Jesus to the world outside of Christendom. Just as the first (Jewish) believers were slow to engage in the fulfilment of the great commission, the nineteenth century Western church was slow to accept the missionary movement.

Just like the first missionaries took their Jewish cultural practices along with them, so the modern missionaries took with them their European Christianity, their European cultural forms and patterns of practice. It was right that they did, in that they were European. But just as the first missionaries learned not to expect their Gentile converts to adopt their Jewish practices, the European missionaries had to learn not to expect their converts to adopt European practices as if they were an essential part of the gospel or the only way to outwork it.

I remember as a young varsity student spending three months helping missionaries in New Guinea. The New Guinean highlanders were experiencing the first generation of contact with Europeans. On one occasion some newly converted New Guineans approached some missionaries, requesting a Christian wedding. Some inexperienced missionaries tried to source such things as a white gown for the young bride. As a youth I did not overtly question the missionaries, but I thought to myself that these missionaries had missed it. They had confused European Christian traditions with the essence of what it means to enter a covenant marriage relationship with the Lord. I thought, and I still do, that they should have discussed with the family the biblical principles of marriage and sought from them the best way to express those principles in their own cultural context.

The first of the modern missionaries had no experience or even theoretical training in cross-cultural communication. At first they had little idea that they were being 'read' in the framework of thought and practice of an entirely different culture. The apostle Paul, though thoroughly Jewish in a Jewish cultural setting such as in Jerusalem, had learned to eat with and relate to Gentiles in a non-Jewish manner. He confronted Peter when he failed to do this.[108] Paul related the gospel using the ideas and stories that Gentiles were familiar with to connect them to the gospel.[109] So too, these nineteenth and twentieth century missionaries had to learn to relate to the people using the cultural forms, metaphors and stories with which their hearers were familiar. The story of Hudson Taylor illustrates this well. He realised that he needed to adopt Chinese cultural forms, such as his dress, if he were to effectively communicate the gospel. Just as the practices of the first century missionaries were controversial back in Jerusalem, so too the practices of the missionaries who were learning these cross-cultural principles were vigorously questioned back in Europe and America. Back at 'home' their supporters had little idea of the cross-cultural dimension of their task.

These missionaries came with a set of Christian cultural forms

---

108. Galatians 2:11-14
109. e.g. Acts 17

– patterns of practice they were used to in Europe. In time they learned that a different set of practices could be equally apt in fulfilling the heart of the Gospel.

Some missionaries learnt these lessons well and released their converts to express their faith in their own cultural way. As a result indigenous movements could flourish. Others struggled to trust their converts in this way. In this case the gospel became mixed with the imposition of cultural forms, usually European. Yet the Lord still blessed their work, because the gospel is still the power of God to save even when it is mixed with a dose of cultural legalism.

Cultural desecration?

Western observers and historians, who perceive Christianity to be merely a religion, that is, a set of cultural forms imposed on to believers, have been critical of the missionary movement. They interpret the work of missionaries as a desecration of the indigenous cultures. To the degree that European missionaries did impose their European practices, they are right. But, as we have said before, the gospel of Christ is about the transformation of people's hearts, not the enforced transmission of cultural practices. When the gospel of Christ is truly engaged, the transformed hearts, minds and attitudes of believers will be worked out into changes of the culture in a way that is likely to be peculiar to the context of the local culture.

In his book '*The Cross-cultural Process in Christian History*',[110] Andrew Walls devotes a chapter to the story of Samuel Ajayi Crowther, an African Christian leader whose life spanned the nineteenth century. He emerged in a missionary environment where mostly the cross-cultural lessons had not yet been learned. For many, the priority was to teach English to render the local languages unnecessary. But Crowther was a pioneer not locked in this

---

110. Walls (2002, pp. 155-164)

mindset. He was the first African to lead a team in the translation of the Bible into a local language. With personal integrity, graciousness and godliness, he established and led a significant indigenous movement in the land along the River Niger in what is now Nigeria. He practiced the principle of indigenisation. The leadership was indigenous. The cultural forms were indigenous. The theological emphases were African. This was all very controversial with the European based missionary movement. There was enormous tension between the two factions particularly when the succession to his leadership was in question. However, his legacy has born much fruit in the succeeding generations and has been a factor in the indigenisation of African Christianity that we see today.

In recent decades the move to seriously study the cultural dimension of missiology and to be intentional in cross-cultural evangelism and teaching has contributed to a dramatic indigenisation of the church in the non-western world. This is discussed in the chapter about the contemporary global challenge.

To study and discuss

1. Choose a part of the world, maybe your own country, and investigate early indigenous Christian movements.
- How did the culturally European church cope with them?
- Did they regard them as in error?
- On what criteria did they 'judge' them?
- Can you identify the issues to do with cultural forms and those to do with basic doctrine?

CULTURE IN TODAY'S WORLD

Effecting Cultural Change in the Contemporary World

As in other times, in the past century the process of passing on the cultural forms of Christianity while losing the heart of the gospel has often been a feature of Western culture. It has been accelerated by influential church leaders who have abandoned a biblical world-view and the core truths of the gospel.

Patterns of practice have become disconnected from their Christian roots. The celebration of Christmas is a classic example. Many of the cultural forms of Christmas have non-Christian origins. When Europe was infiltrated by Christianity, these forms were progressively 'redeemed'. They were given Christian meaning and intermingled with practices of Christian origin. In the twentieth century, many Westerners became 'secular' in their thinking but still clung to celebrating Christmas. The rationale for this practice became ideas about celebrating family instead of Christ. In recent decades, public displays of overtly Christian forms such as nativity scenes have been frowned on and in some cases banned. Consequently, Christian patterns of practice have often been confined to the privacy of church and Christian home.

The contemporary Western world tends to see Christianity as a religion to be tolerated along with other religions. It is regarded as a marginalised sub-culture, and as such is irrelevant to the real world and basically ineffectual. While it merely presents itself as an alternative set of practices that can be personally adhered to, it can be lived with provided it does not declare it has some universal truth that applies to non-believers.

But if Christianity presents itself as an alternative worldview, as it did in the New Testament times, it is declared to be foolishness.[111] And if the Christian worldview is declared to be universal truth and thus is the only way, it is considered to be more than harmlessly amusing. It is considered dangerous, just like it was in Roman times. This is the stance of the new wave of articulate atheists in the West. Real Christianity reaches into a deeper level than that at which the antagonists of the gospel have often examined their own lives. The unexamined foundations of their thought patterns are being threatened. The gospel is the ultimate inconvenient truth.

Christianity is not an alternative culture. The gospel is not just different practices. The message of the cross is working from a whole different set of presuppositions. It is a subversive philosophy of life. It has the ability to change from within any culture, sometimes confronting while sometimes supporting cultural elements in a society. It has the ability to transform a culture.

As citizens of an eternal Kingdom we have been set free from the bondage of the confines of a particular earthly culture. Amongst other things, spiritual maturity involves realising this in our hearts – stepping into this freedom in Christ. Yet as ambassadors of the Kingdom we are planted in this world to relate to and be agents of change in earthly cultures. We find ourselves in a world of people locked into cultures, in both forms and their foundations. How do we be part of Christ's culture transforming process? For example, what do we do when a practice exhibited by the world clearly is contrary to the attitudes and practices advocated by Christ? What should we Christians do when public funds are used for abortion on demand, or when a practice of sensuality promoting sexual immorality is publicly imposed on our society?

---

111. 1 Corinthians 1:18ff

Do we yearn for the former familiar culture? This traditionalism is missing the real issues lying at the base of the cultural changes occurring, and achieves nothing but despair. Do we withdraw from the fray and ignore the issues of the day? Such a stance confirms the world's stereotype of Christians – fundamentalists who don't have a clue about the real issues. Do we stand on the sidelines and be confrontational? This is a recipe for how to make enemies and not influence them. Or do we get Christians into politics running the government so we solve the world's problems – political triumphalism? All of these approaches can be observed in our generation. Some of us have been involved in varying degrees in some of them.

I suggest the Bible outlines three steps in our involvement toward transforming a culture. They are:

- **Connecting** to the culture,
- **Confronting** the culture, and
- **Converting** the culture.

Connecting to the culture

This I call the *'incarnational'* step. If we want to make a difference in the culture in which we have been planted, we need to become familiar with:

1) the patterns of practice, the cultural forms
2) the language of the culture, including the metaphors and the idioms used by the people in the culture
3) the thought patterns and worldview which underpin the culture.

Even if we have grown up and lived in the culture in question, we do well to intentionally make an effort to understand the worldview existent in the culture to enable us to make connection with it. Then we can identify concepts, metaphors and parables which act as stepping stones or bridges for communicating the truth of the gospel.

Much of what was said about the life of Jesus in chapter 5 illustrates this principle of incarnation. Jesus earned the listening ears of the Jewish community by living as a Jew and speaking in the terms of the Jews.

Wonderful examples of this incarnational mode of connecting to the people of a culture are found throughout scripture and Christian history. One dramatic and extreme example of this in recent history is that of Bruce Olsen who lost himself in the culture of a remote South American tribe, previously untouched by outsiders.[112] Not surprisingly, his life story is controversial.

When you realise that the cultural forms are neutral in themselves, you can contemplate intentionally practising cultural forms that you would not naturally do, in order to win people to Christ. As Paul said, "I have become all things to all men so that by all means possible I might save some."[113] Remember, as was noted earlier, when God was communicating His truth to the Israelites He used familiar cultural forms with a significant difference. The critical discernment is not how they were similar, but how, in their similarity, they were radically different. Similarly, it is quite feasible to live in a Hindu community and intentionally and overtly practice meditation so that they might identify with you. You would be 'talking their language'. Rather than be repulsed by your foreign ways, they may observe your practice and detect a difference. When they ask questions, you can explain how you meditate on the Lord, His Word, who He is and what He has done in your life and indeed for them. Then there is a real possibility that faith in Christ will be attractive to them as it can be understood and practised in a truly Indian way.

---

112. Olsen (1978)
113. 1 Corinthians 9:19-23

Confronting the culture

This is the *'being light'* aspect. In order to confront, we must demonstrate the way it is done in the Kingdom of God. The community of Christ will develop its unique culture as an outworking of the gospel. This is being a 'prophetic voice' by real life action. The fruits of the Kingdom will speak for themselves. We confront the culture by demonstrating a similar but radically different culture. Corporately, this may take the form of a Christian welfare organisation, a Christian school, a Christian sports team or arts group, a business, or any other enterprise. Individually, it may take form by the way you care for your work colleagues, the way you manage your money, or the way you love your family. The context and the call of God will determine the shape of your 'lamp' in the community.

Being light necessitates getting our act together. The Christian community has not earned the right to harangue the world about the breakdown in family, when the record for Christian families is no better than that of the world. We must demonstrate in deed how to be faithful spouses, effective parents and business men and women with integrity and acumen. Being light means we show the world how it can be done right.

Then when invited, and within the confines of expediency, we can verbalise the difference as an apologetic to the world. Jesus' polemic applied to the Pharisees came in the context of their reaction to His patterns of practice – Jewish, but with a difference, which they observed and sometimes objected to. The language He used in confronting the Jewish religious leaders was *their* language – the idioms and metaphors of the culture He was criticising. When confronting the issues of the day we need to express ourselves, not in 'Christianese', but in the words and concepts that the world will understand. As we often say in relating to the contemporary Western world, we need to think Biblically and speak secularly.

131

It must be emphasised that we cannot stand in judgment from a position outside of the culture. We are not qualified to confront until we enter the culture and truly identify with those in the culture and are invited to speak. Recently I was in conversation with a dear friend who was criticising an iconic feature of New Zealand Maori culture, the haka. The national sports teams use this 'war dance' before doing battle in the match. She said it was unredeemable and should be abolished. I attempted to defend Maori culture by proposing that some Christian Maori could compose (as they have) a haka that expresses a different attitude – one of friendship and love. Afterwards I realised I did not engage in the conversation well. I should have reminded her that neither of us was qualified to judge as we are not Maori nor have lived as Maori.

In 1 Corinthians, the apostle Paul addressed the issue of sexual immorality in the church.[114] He said it was serious and needed to be confronted following principles of relationships as Jesus taught. If the persons were unrepentant he advised the church to exclude them from the fellowship, so that God could deal with them as He would unbelievers. Paul did not then tell the church to harangue them once they were outside the fellowship. In fact he wrote, "What business is it of mine to judge those outside the church? ... God will judge those outside."[115]

If we publicly harangue unbelievers who practice evil we will be misunderstood. The world sees us as wanting to impose our religion, that is, our cultural practices on them. They will not see our heart of genuine concern. The New Testament does not instruct us to confront head-on the people professing no faith in God and who are locked in an ungodly culture, especially when uninvited. Neither does the practice of the apostles in the story in the New Testament show examples of such confrontation. Rather, we confront by the

---

114. 1 Corinthians 5
115. 1 Corinthians 5:12

example of our lives and the proclamation of the gospel.

Paul's letter to Philemon illustrates his approach. In this case the issue was slavery. The culture of the ancient world was dependent on a system of slavery. People were either born a slave or a free person. It was grossly unfair. From our perspective, where we live in a culture that now despises such inequity, we have no problems seeing it is wrong. But in those days a demonstration against slavery would be totally misunderstood. It would be tantamount to treason. Paul did not publicly preach against slavery, but he preached that in Christ there was neither 'slave nor free".[116]

Onesimus was Philemon's slave. He had run away, breaking his contract, albeit a contract that he possibly never agreed to but had imposed upon him by birth. He headed for the 'big smoke', Rome, and somehow he met up with Paul who was in prison there. He was now repentant and won to Christ. Philemon, the offended master was Paul's brother in Christ. So now Paul, Philemon and Onesimus were all brothers in Christ. This equality in relationship to God now had to be worked out in practice in this world. The culture of the world would have pressured Philemon to exercise retribution and to impose severe bondage if not death on the dissident slave. The gospel of Christ was clearly pushing against the culture.

Paul did not tell Onesimus to assert his rights. Neither did Paul assert some official authority on Philemon. Such actions would be akin to the spirit of this world. They were operating in a different kingdom, a kingdom which encouraged servant leadership. The rule of Christ was not to come by political or social force. Instead Paul attempted to persuade Philemon to see the implications of their mutual inner transformation, their new relationship as brothers in Christ.[117] The love of Christ inside the men was to be worked out in action. The culture of slavery was to be undermined from the

---

116. Galatians 3:28
117. The 'book' Philemon

inside out, and this was to begin within the community of believers themselves showing a different way.

When instructing slaves about their attitude to their masters, the Apostle Peter insists that they obey them even in the face of suffering injustice at their hand. He cites Christ's suffering as an example to follow.[118] Clearly, within the context they found themselves, expediency demanded no overt rocking of the cultural boat, but a covert infiltration of truth.

This principle of influencing from the inside out is illustrated by Peter's instructions to the wives to whom he was writing.[119] The subordination of women was entrenched in the thinking and practice of the culture of the day, but the gospel of Christ declared equality – that in Christ there is neither male nor female.[120] This truth was the foundation for the emancipation of women.

The gist of Peter's message to them was that wives could be influential, not by asserting their rights as equals in the Lord, but by working out their inner transformation. The work of God could have influence if they let the beauty of the spirit be enhanced, rather than overshadowed, by their outward appearance. By instructing them to be submissive, Peter did not imply that wives were inferior, or that the existing social order was right. Affronting the culture would not win unbelieving men. Rather, they could be influential by working out the power of the spirit from the inside out.

The cultural change in the Christian community would come by the work of Christ inside first. The rule of Christ begins on the inside. You change in the heart first. You show that change by your life. One by one they see you change. They want what you have. You share the good news. They change. And so the 'snow ball effect' will continue. Eventually you have an avalanche – the transformation of a whole culture. Being light has now become being salt too.

118. 1 Peter 3:18ff
119. 1 Peter 3:3ff
120. Galatians 3:28

Converting the culture

This is the *'being salt'* aspect. Cultural transformation motivated by Christ is to be done by *subversion* not compulsion. It will not be achieved by firstly changing the structures of society against the will of the people. Rather the internal motivations of the people need to be changed. The people need to be changed. The converting power of the gospel works 'inside out'. This takes time (sometimes more than one generation) and patient communication of the gospel and its application to the issues facing the culture, and then providing positive, practical and palatable alternatives to the current pattern of practice. These alternatives can often come straight from scripture – for example, by examining practices instituted by God in the Old Testament, discerning the underlying principles and then applying them to the contemporary situation.

In the late eighteenth and early nineteenth centuries in Britain, William Wilberforce faced the slavery issue. Slavery on the basis of race was entrenched in the attitudes, not just the practice, of the culture. The abolition of slavery required more than a mere change in legislation.

The surrounding culture can blind us to the truth. We can even look sincerely into God's Word and still miss seeing what we are really like. When the slave trader John Newton met Christ in a storm in the middle of the ocean, he did not think to abandon his 'profession'. He was blinded by his culture to the evils of his practice. But God had begun the work of His kingdom on the man's heart. It took years of the work of the Spirit in his heart to awaken him to reform his practice. Eventually he could say, with regard to the slave trade, "I was blind, but now I see".[121]

Now, influenced by John Newton, Wilberforce applied himself

---

121. The words of the well known hymn, Amazing Grace, were written by John Newton (1725-1807).

to the task of legislatively abolishing the institution of slavery. He did not harass the slave traders themselves. He set about persuading the people of Britain and in particular the members of Parliament, the majority of whom claimed to be Christians, that slavery was an evil abomination and should be abolished. At times he was tempted to compromise his ethics to accomplish his goal, but encouraged by his fellow believers, he trusted God rather than using the practices of the kingdom of this world. Wilberforce was admired by members on both sides of parliament for his ethical principles and his balanced principled views of the various issues before parliament. Eventually truth prevailed and a measure of the Kingdom of God was achieved in the nation's culture. The slave trade and eventually slavery itself was legally abolished in Great Britain.

The inside out approach

A significant issue in contemporary Western culture is our infatuation with things. The rampant materialism of the Western world is so pervasive that many of the citizens of God's Kingdom are blinded to it. How can we affect the materialistic consumerism of our culture? Make the rich feel guilty or rob the rich to pay the poor? That is the method of the world. Whether done illegally or legally through taxes, the end result is virtually no effect on the inequity in our society. The affluence gap just gets bigger while the hearts of the rich are unchanged.

Christ must change our hearts on this first. The Spirit must take away our blindness that we have inherited from the surrounding culture. It sometimes takes believers in another culture to observe us and alert us to our blindness. Our involvement with Christians of another culture and their involvement with us help us be alerted to our own cultural lens. Then we must let this be worked out in our own lives practically. The signs of the Kingdom in this regard will most likely include a simplification of our lifestyle to generate funds to facilitate the helping of the poor. James' 'true religion' will be seen. In this way we will be salt and light, infiltrating our culture with a new way of approaching the issue.

Whatever the issue, we must not think that the problem will be solved by electing a Christian government that will enact 'Christian' legislation. That methodology is the methodology of the kingdoms of this world. It is working from the assumption that the problem is the social system and structures, and that the state through correct legislation can fix it. The basic problem is not the socio-economic structures, and the state is not the agent of salvation. The heart of the problem is the heart of humans. The answer lies firstly with fixing the inner intents of human hearts.

> The solution is for individuals to turn away from their individual acts of disobedience. With the help of God's grace, this will lead to a change in the way they relate to others. When enough people do this on a large scale, the alteration of social relations leads to a cultural reformation.[122]

That is why Christ is the Saviour and the human agents of change for good (salvation) are us, His church, not the state.

The reformer Martin Luther taught that we should engage the culture in which we live. He taught that Christ could and should be followed in our public life, but suggested that the rules to be followed, the civil laws, were independent of Christian or church law.

Richard John Neuhaus wrote,

> ...the church ...must maintain a critical distance from all the

---

122. Flannagan, Matthew, in The Left is not Right, in *Reality Magazine*, Issue 35 (1999)

kingdoms of the world, whether actual or proposed. Christians betray their Lord if, in theory or practice, they equate the kingdom of God with any political, social or economic order of this passing time. At best, such orders permit the proclamation of the gospel of the Kingdom and approximate, in small part, the freedom, peace, and justice for which we hope.[123]

Niebuhr put it this way:

Christ… cleanses the springs of action… He does not directly govern the external actions or construct the immediate community in which man carries out His work.[124]

The Fundamentalist movement tended to focus on the salvation of the inner person alone, to the detriment of the essential outworking of it into all of life. Recognising this error, the 'moral right' movement attempted to effect godly change by gaining legislative and judicial power. As the salt of the earth in a nation with a democratic aspect to its constitution, the Christian community must engage our culture in the realm of politics, but never entertain grand illusions of a Christian government saving the world with Christian laws. We cannot afford to have utopian ideas about our involvement in politics. That is not the plan of the Kingdom!

In the '70s a young man called Tony Blair was studying at Oxford.[125] Like many students of his time he related to a group of students who theorised about how they could 'save the world'. Under the influence of Peter Thomson, an Anglican priest from Melbourne, they discussed the philosophy of John Macmurray and discussed how best to achieve the goals of socialism. The alternatives of revolution or social and political changes through legislation

123. Neuhaus (1981)
124. Niebuhr (1951), p174, 175(1951, pp. 174-175)
125. Rentoul (1997), p39-47

were considered. They came to recognise that such alternatives were doomed to fail unless there was a change in the internal motivations of the people. It was at this time that Tony chose to attend confirmation classes. It would seem that he knew that he needed to change on the inside first. This may well explain why later in life Prime Minister Blair never went down the utopian road. He was a socialist with a difference!

The challenge

We are called to make a difference in this world. The change in the cultural forms we may see is not the permanent and ultimate Kingdom of God. That will be seen when Christ comes again. Carson puts it this way:

> Yet it is possible so to focus on the rescue and regeneration of *individuals* that we fail to see the temporary good things we can do to improve even transform some social *structures*... Sometimes a disease can be knocked out; sometimes sex traffic can be considerably reduced; sometimes slavery can be abolished in a region; sometimes more equitable laws can foster justice and reduce corruption; sometimes engagement in the arts can produce wonderful work that inspires a new generation. When such things become part of an inherited set of assumptions passed on to the next generation, they have become part of the culture; they have effected some cultural change. Of course, none of these good things is guaranteed to be enduring; none brings in the consummated kingdom...[126]

As an introduction to the way in which people with Bible in their hearts and practice can make a huge cultural difference, I sug-

---

126. Carson (2008) p217, 218.

gest reading Loren Cunningham's book, *The Book that Transforms Nations*.[127]

And so comes to us the challenge to be involved in not just the redemption of souls but of the cultures in which souls live. As Watkins put it:

> In a society where no public face of faith is easily presented, where the 'religious' is confined to the private and non-rational, what is more and more required is that Christians so embody their faith in the world that this world itself becomes evangelized. So, for example, the evangelizing task of artists, businessmen, those involved in the media – as well as those in teaching – is so to enter into these human cultures, with faith and authenticity, that Christ and his message are made present to these places, both with and without explicit articulation. ... Such embodiment of the gospel is what makes for the evangelization of culture.[128]

As history shows, we can make a significant difference in this world. The love of God compels us to be engaged with the cultures of this world. And, as John Stott says, "'engagement' means turning our faces toward the world in compassion, getting our hands dirty, sore and worn in its service, and feeling deep within us the stirring love of God which cannot be contained."[129]

---

127. Cunningham (2007)
128. Watkins, (2008) p85
129. Stott, (1984) p14

To study and discuss

1. Why is it important that the 'connecting' phase be not overlooked?

2. Read the stories related in Daniel chapters 1, 3 and 6 and find ways in which they illustrate the principles discussed in this chapter.

3. Imagine you are living in a community which practices the cultural forms of one of the world religions.
- What cultural forms could you practice which would help them relate to you?
- How in your very similar practice would you consciously do things differently to convey the truth of the gospel?

4. The Western world has seen the change of laws which used to respect the sanctity of marriage. Marriage is now seen as one option of expressing a relationship as the basis of family.
- In what ways can Christians be 'light' in this context?
- In what ways can we be 'salt' in regard to this issue?
- When is it appropriate for us to confront the world on this issue?
- How should we shape our language to do this?

SIXTEEN

Multiculturalism and Biculturalism

In this chapter I have used examples from the South Pacific. Stories from around the globe can equally well illustrate the principles addressed.

The natural tendency of a people group is to be secure in its culture and to want to protect that culture as one protects the secure fortress of the home. The people of a culture under threat will resort to various means to secure their fortress.

One method is to lash out and eliminate all people of a different culture from their territory. This has been called 'ethnic cleansing' in recent years. This insidious response to cultural insecurity has caused the suffering and death of millions.

Another response has been to gain political power and give your culture a privileged position. The islands of Fiji were populated by the indigenous Melanesian Fijian people. Many had been responsive to the gospel of Christ. Ensuing generations had in large embraced a cultural Christianity. The British colonial occupants brought in Indian workers to work in the coffee plantations. When Fiji was made an independent democratic nation in the early '70s, the Indian people were fast becoming the majority. Some Christian observers in the '70s suggested that possible troubles lay ahead because most of the Fijian Christians had not reached out across the cultural gap to the Hindu and Muslim Indian population. When in the '80s the government was for the first time reflecting the Indian majority, some of the Fijians reacted to protect their culture. The political coup that followed was motivated by the insecurity of a people whose culture was under threat. It was given 'Christian' justification. It was the first of a series of coups that have occurred in Fiji since.[130]

Sometimes the majority culture with the power of the state will forbid the minority culture from practicing their cultural forms, or anyone of the majority group from changing to another pattern of practice. Islamic governments often do this. In New Zealand seventy years ago, Maori children were forbidden to speak Maori in the confines of the school. Yes, English is a more useful language on the international scene, but attempting to eliminate a culture by banning the use of its language not only will create a justified response of anger, but is contrary to the purposes of God. On the whole it would seem the Maori population reacted to this gross hegemony with admirable dignity.

Biculturalism

In subsequent decades, it has been recognised that New Zealand is the only place in the world where we can expect Maori culture to be preserved and continue to develop. The government of New Zealand has developed a policy of 'biculturalism'. Both English and Maori are official languages of New Zealand. Bilingual and Maori speaking educational institutions (particularly early childhood and elementary schools) have been established. Serious effort involving significant amounts of time and finance has and is being made to redress historical inequities. The spirit of this is (or should be) entirely compatible with the spirit of reconciliation and unity expressed in the New Testament. What occurs 'behind closed doors'

130. We have cause to rejoice that in recent years, despite the political scene appearing to be more sinister, a move of repentance, reconciliation and healing has begun. See Cunningham L, (2007, pp. 211-215)

may sometimes be otherwise. The methods being used have inevitably been a mixture of the methods of the Kingdom of God and the kingdoms of this world. Christians of both ethnicities enjoy the challenge of promoting the methods of the Kingdom of Christ in this bicultural context.

The board room at the Christian school where I have an office was being prepared for a meeting. I asked the person doing the preparation of the room what meeting was happening. I was told, "The cultural committee". Thinking about the various expressions of a Christian school's culture, I decided to ask what the cultural committee was responsible for. "You know, the cultural things", was the reply. Well, I didn't know, so I asked who was on the committee. Most of the membership was Maori, so I realised this committee concerned itself with things Maori that happened on the campus. I think it is very appropriate that a Christian school in New Zealand should ensure that such activities are consistent with their biblical Christian mission and also be in harmony with the culture of the people such activities are honouring. The curious thing to me was that the committee was not called 'the Maori protocol committee' or even 'the bicultural committee'. The name of the committee reflected that in the thinking of many New Zealanders, 'cultural' has come to mean 'taha Maori', things Maori. It is encouraging that biculturalism has a significant profile in the community, but a little disturbing that 'culture' seems to only apply to Maoridom. No wonder some non-Maori ask the question, "Don't I have a culture?" Of course they have a culture. We are all cultural beings.

But, as believers set free from the bondage of yearning for self-fulfilment, we should not be focused on ourselves and our culture, but on others. It is not about claiming our rights but about affording others theirs. When it comes to cultural forms, it is not our personal cultural sensitivity but that of the other we should consider.[131] It is

---

131. 1 Corinthians 10:28, 29

about honouring others. In the racist regimes in Africa last century, what caused many black people to feel the most pain was not the political oppression but the dishonour, disrespect and humiliation thrust upon them by the attitudes of many white people.

Moving our focus from preserving our own culture to honouring others of a different culture is an aspect of our original purpose to reflect the nature of God. The focus of each member of the Trinity is other centred. The Father defers the work of creation to the Spirit and the Word. The Son reveals and glorifies the Father. The Spirit speaks of the Son. They give witness of each other.[132] Humans reflect the Godhead by honouring one another by helping the other to excel in what they do well. So too, in the cross cultural sense, we reflect the nature of God as we honour one another.

Referring to the cultural traditions of the Pharisees and scribes, Jesus quoted from Isaiah saying, "These people honour me with their lips, but their hearts are far from me."[133] He was saying it must start with our heart attitude. The core problem is lack of respect and honour in our hearts. Cultural reconciliation must start with valuing the other person or people highly – in our heart. If we go through the bicultural process without this there will never be unity.

Once we have our attitude right, then this inner attitude can be expressed, and observed by others. Firstly, we express honour by our words and speech. As the scripture encourages us, our speech should build *others* up. Gracious speech will consider the conscience and hence the culture of the *other*. It is most honouring when we use *their* language. Secondly, we can use gestures which *they* will read as honouring. Once again, the cultural forms of the recipient need to be considered. Thirdly, we honour by giving – giving things *they* would value. And finally, we honour by acts of service. We need to ask what will help others fulfil *their* goals, and then do that.

---

132. Genesis 1:1-3, John 14:8-17, John 16:13-15, 1 John 5:7-9
133. Mark 7:5ff

Honour is a two way thing[134] especially in a bicultural context. It begins with, and is dependent on, the heart attitude, which is then worked out by culturally determined action and speech. The ever-present temptation is to make cultural practices the centre of the issue. For many our identity is solely based on our prestige in the community or our cultural heritage, be it our genealogy or artefacts our families possess. As my family name suggests I have a Viking and English heritage. In my family tree there are notable Englishmen including some prime ministers. I like the idea, and enjoy telling people about my family history, but it all pales into insignificance when I consider that in Christ I am a child of God. As Paul said that these things he considered loss for Christ.[135] My identity is based on that immediate relationship to Him.

Christians need to recognise the key issues are those of the heart. We have been liberated from finding our identity solely in 'our culture'. Ideally, Christians of any culture should be able not to take offense because of 'cultural insensitivity'. Our identity is found in our relationship to God in Christ. Our acts should be moved by the love of Christ in our hearts. Respecting, loving and honouring others by making an effort to span the cultural gap should be at the heart of the way we respond to others with a different cultural heritage.

In reality most New Zealanders of European descent are living a largely monocultural lifestyle interrupted occasionally by events incorporating Maori protocols. Some of the Maori population enjoy a bicultural lifestyle, and a few live mono-culturally as Maori. It is mostly Maori who have to tolerate the disrespect and cultural intolerance of some other New Zealanders. It behoves Christians to not be part of this disrespect.

---

134. This is expressed well by Garry McDonald, (2008, Introduction)
135. Philippians 3:3-9

Multiculturalism

Added to this mix is the dynamic of the cultures of a great variety of further immigrants to the nation. In this respect New Zealand is like any other contemporary Western nation. The biblical principles applicable to cross-cultural and multicultural contexts outlined in this book become a pressing practical challenge without us crossing any international borders.

In all of this the ideal of multiculturalism bears upon us. Underlying this concept of multiculturalism are two debatable ideas.

The first idea is that all cultures are equal and equally above criticism. This idea comes in part from confusing culture or ethnicity with race. As discussed in chapter one, a people's culture is not predetermined by their genes. This idea also stems from moral relativism, a mindset totally in conflict with biblical revelation. The reality from a biblical perspective is that cultural forms in themselves are neutral, but all forms flow out of a spring of ideas, attitudes and values which are never neutral. Every culture is *infected* and *affected* by ideas which come from God or from the prince of this world. The gospel needs to connect with, react to and subvert all cultures. Some cultures have a long history of this interaction. That does not necessarily make them superior, but often it brings the blessings of the knowledge of God to the people. When we are tempted to judge the people of another culture we do well to remind ourselves that God is judge and we don't need to do His job! The principles of scripture already outlined in this book are most applicable in this scenario.

The second debatable idea is that a multi-ethnic community can function coherently. The communication challenges, both verbal and non-verbal, are huge. The cry heard in many Western nations experiencing the frustrations that come from this mix of many cultures is, "Where has common sense gone?" Common sense is now not common because the community does not share a common worldview! The reality may well be that multiculturalism won't work this side of the general resurrection.

However, the Christian community should stand out as light in this world. In Christ, the walls of separation have been broken down. We share the mindset of Christ. We have common foundations of thought derived from the revelation of scripture. We are compelled by the love of Christ. If we recognise our freedom from the obligations of imposed cultural forms, we as children of God have the best chance of all humans to make it work. Recently, we were chatting to the proprietor of a local Indian restaurant. He is a fellow believer who has migrated from India. He was describing the wonderful example his home church in Kolkata was to the community. He said that in his church there were a great variety of people: Hindus, Muslims, Sikhs, Englishmen and Americans. What he meant was that they all loved the Lord and each other and yet maintained many cultural practices of the traditions from whence they came. The people of Kolkata are mostly Hindus. Hindus value diversity and faithfulness to the culture of your upbringing. As a result this church was a wonderful witness to the unity that comes in Christ to the mostly Hindu community of Kolkata. The unity of the Spirit can be worked out in practice.

A close-knit multicultural community may result in a mutual assimilation of cultures, so that the ensuing generations are moving toward a new monocultural community with a merged local culture. But hopefully it would in turn be actively embracing more members from diverse cultural backgrounds.

Mono-ethnic subcultures

In nations where there is a high degree of personal liberty, an increasing reality is the development of a variety of sub-cultures in a mono-ethnic community. These include sub-cultures based on religious beliefs and traditions, socio-economic status, age group, special artistic or sporting interests, and even criminal activity. Cross-cultural interaction with all its challenges is unavoidable.

It was the age of Beatlemania and rock and roll. Our church youth group was very evangelistic in outlook. Every Saturday night was an opportunity for an evangelistic rally. We held western nights, Hawaiian nights, minstrel nights, quiz nights – you name it – all to draw a crowd and preach the gospel. Some weekends we would go to a small country town and hold our rally there in support of the local church. We would do some street preaching during the day and a rally at night. On this occasion in the middle of summer we were at a seaside town about 2 hours from our home city. All was going to plan until we began to set up for the evening rally. The local pastor's wife saw us setting up the drums, and 'all hell' broke loose. "You are not going to play drums! That is the devil's music. Drumming comes from witchcraft in Africa. We are not going to drum up demons in our church!" Whoa! We had not struck this before – well not quite as hostile as this! We sat down and prayed. We decided to go ahead – without drums. We thought it would sound pathetic to the youth of the town we were trying to reach, but we had to trust God to use our sacrifice to Him.

On reflecting back, it was clear that our parents' generation had hardly experienced anything but European style music, and any-thing else was spooky to them, so must be of the devil. Rock, with its roots back to Africa through America must be evil. We realise now that every generation tends to identify their cultural forms with what must be good. And Christians can contort it even fur-ther and give their cultural forms ultimate value. Thank God, Jesus came to save us from cultural bondage.

Today the challenge still remains – within a 'mono-ethnic' local church there are sub-cultures based on age and cultural tastes. It is disappointing to see Christians quibbling over cultural forms such as styles of music, tattoos, clothing styles, body piercing, and the role of women in the church, instead of being concerned about the matters of the heart, reaching the lost and meeting real social needs. Sadly, for some of us we have to get to an age where we have to tolerate the young generation's music in church before we realise we have confused our cultural tastes with our faith in Christ.

In the 1970s school teachers in Australia were expected to wear jackets and ties. Simon was called to a meeting with the principal and board chairman. He figured what it was about. Simon was a youth during the days of flower power. When he turned his life over to Jesus in 1968, the Lord delivered him from his drug addiction and turned his life around. He had gone from strength to strength in his relationship with Jesus. He had a rich worship life. He was now in his fifth year as a teacher in this school. The new principal was great but had insisted that he wear a tie when he was teaching. He had repeatedly 'forgotten' to conform. And so, now he was about to be 'given the hard word' – all because the principal wanted him to conform to his petty rules.

At the meeting he was reminded of the dress code for teachers and that the school's community expected him to dress formally and with dignity. He insisted that a tie was not reasonable as he was not comfortable with formal dress. He said, "It's not my culture."

As a Christian who had been entrusted with the responsibility of teaching children, what principles should be guiding his decision on this matter of culture? Was the school community locked into a form of cultural legalism? The school leadership should be considering the changing cultural forms in its community. Does this justify Simon's stand? Our friend Simon needed to be considering not 'my culture' but the culture of the families he was serving.

We see in our modern cities many Christians seeking out a

'church' in which they feel comfortable. This usually means one in which the cultural forms are familiar and the people meet their needs. They have missed the purpose of the body of Christ. Their purpose in 'doing church' should be something like building others up, encouraging them in the faith and complementing them in service. The cultural forms that make you feel comfortable should not come into it. It should be the cultural forms of the people you want to edify or reach that matter. In fact, when your mission is other-related, 'church' should often be uncomfortable.

Let us learn to reflect our unity in the Lord, and celebrate our diversity, by being other-centred in all that we do.

We live in a time that offers a great array of opportunities to apply the principles of the Kingdom of God. Let us embrace these opportunities with enthusiasm.

To study and discuss

1. Revise previous chapters to answer this question:
What are the 'principles of the Kingdom of God' directly applicable to the bicultural or multicultural settings in which we find ourselves?

2. Revisit the section in chapter four about immigration.
Are there principles to be learned from this story and applied to modern immigration?

3. How does your church educate the youth to reach out to others who are not involved in their youth sub-culture?

4. In a large modern city there are often found some congregations with members from a variety of ethnic backgrounds, and in the same city there are mono-ethnic congregations. Discuss the advantages and disadvantages of both these types of congregations.

SEVENTEEN

The Contemporary Global Challenge

The world is experiencing a startling change in our generation. The face of Christianity is changing dramatically.

For centuries Christianity has been considered by outside observers as a European or Western religion. The patterns of practice described as Christian and observed by outsiders have mostly developed over the centuries in Europe and the West. Western missionaries have gone into the rest of the world and taken their cultural forms along with the gospel. Many Africans, Asians and others have resisted receiving the gospel because it has been seen as an attempt to foist European culture on them.

For generations many indigenous converts have tried to copy the European patterns of practice. These cultural forms tended to become the norms of Christianity. Instead of the gospel of Christ defining Christianity, European or semi-European cultural forms defined what Christianity was all about. I reflect on some African Christians who visit New Zealand and cringe when they experience expressions of Christian faith in Maori cultural forms. While rightly rejecting the animist beliefs and practices out of which many cultural forms have come, they have come to believe that European cultural forms are the only Christian ones. Practising only European cultural forms in Christian meetings reinforces the idea that Christianity is a European religion.

But during the twentieth century, and especially in the latter half of the century, the Christian mission movement became far more intentional in strategies to make connection with the local cultures. Missionaries sought out local metaphors and parables to use in relating the gospel. Seeing the way in which Asian or African recipients of Christianity merely incorporated Christ into their fallacious worldview, missionaries began to see the need to dismantle the local worldview and build an understanding of the biblical story. Many more foreign mission leaders caught on to the need to indigenise the local leadership. Once the indigenous leadership had a biblical worldview, the foreign missionaries could confidently release the leadership. At last they began to trust the locals to translate the gospel in their own cultural contexts.

The result is the emergence of many more African, Asian and other cultural expressions of the gospel. At the risk of doctrinal syncretism arising, western missionaries have allowed local theological emphases to reflect the thinking of the local people.

With the gospel now showing a face that matches the local culture, many more people are receptive to its message. There is a huge influx of converts. For example, for the first time in history many African Muslims are receptive to the gospel. An African Christianity appeals to and connects with Africans more than an Arabic Islam. In our generation the majority of Christians globally has changed. The 'source culture' has been numerically overtaken by the 'receiving cultures'. Asian and African churches are sending missionaries and teachers to the West! This reciprocal ministry of Asian and African missions to the West has great potential to enrich and rejuvenate Western Christianity and may well help save it from its current decline.

This dramatic change mirrors the change that occurred in the church as recorded in the book of Acts. As described in previous chapters, when the church decided to not be biased toward Jewish cultural forms, Gentile Christians soon outnumbered Jewish

Christians, and their theology of Christ emphasised understandings that related to patterns of Greek thinking. For example, Christ was referred to as the Logos and as Lord rather than Son of Man – the same ultimate truth, but in Greek terminology.

Just as the first Jewish Christians initially viewed these changes with scepticism, so too some caring Western Christians fear that the gospel could get lost in a wave of syncretic thought. This is an understandable fear. The first Jewish Christians feared the gentilisation of the faith. They feared that some of the fundamental ideas of the nature and purposes of God would be lost, while not seeing that they themselves had a Jewish bias when it came to the language of theology and the patterns of practice expressing the faith. We Western Christians need to realise that our Christianity is a result of thousands of years of syncretism. Our theological language and other cultural forms are a result of the interaction of the gospel with various European cultures over the years. Our gospel may be pure and biblical but our Christian cultural forms (the patterns of practice we follow) are syncretic.

Referring to Lesslie Newbigin's writings[136] Walls writes:

Western Christians, Newbigin argued, need African and Asian and Hispanic Christians to help them make a Christian analysis of Western culture. Syncretism is a greater peril for Western than for African or Indian Christians and less often recognizable for what it is.

There is a need to identify and distinguish the gospel from our cultural expressions of it, and clearly proclaim the gospel. In cross-cultural contexts we need to be able to proclaim the message in different ways while still maintaining the same message. If all of us discern the difference between the core of the gospel and cultural

---

136. Newbigin (1986). cited by Walls (2001, p. 69)

expressions of it, we will know what to cling on to and to faithfully preserve, while enjoying the freedom to express our faith in a way that sits comfortably within the cultural context.

Paul did not tell his hearers to do everything he did, but rather to follow his example of following Christ.[137] We are to make disciples of Christ, not ourselves. We do well to encourage converts in another culture not to copy our patterns of practice but to copy our commitment to the Lord and His gospel, and to seek the Lord as to how best express and communicate the gospel in their own cultural context. On occasions, our Western practice may well be the best way to do this, but will be replicated in their culture, not as a means to righteousness, but for reasons of expediency.

The ability to discern the difference between the gospel and cultural expressions of it is enhanced by cross-cultural evangelism, teaching and fellowship. This works in two ways. Firstly, to proclaim the gospel faithfully in the 'language' of a different culture necessitates us having a clearer understanding of the gospel itself. Secondly, as we allow our brothers and sisters of another culture to speak into our lives, they can show us where we have confused our cultural biases with the gospel.

It should not be surprising to find that the streams of the church involved most in the missionary movement have become those which are less committed to their specific patterns of practice and more committed to the gospel. It would seem that they have become more centred on Christ and the matters of the heart than being preoccupied with church activities.

In the same way, cross-cultural evangelism, teaching and fellowship may well help us transmit the gospel to our children's generation. The core of the gospel, not just the cultural forms may be handed down to our children. And thus an intergenerational loss of the faith may be stemmed.

---

137. 1 Corinthians 11:1

Reflecting on the trans-generational vulnerability of the Christian faith, Andrew Walls stresses the importance of the cross-cultural process to Christianity:[138]

...cross-cultural diffusion has been necessary to Christianity.

The fact that that cross-cultural diffusion is so characteristic of Christianity leaves the Christian faith with tensions that may be creative or destructive. Cultural diversity is built into the church: so is the ecumenical sharing of its diverse cultural communities.

The suggestion is that significant and deep cross-cultural engagement can act as a protection against cultural legalism and doctrinal syncretism. It is for these reasons that some have suggested that one of the basic signs of a mature Christian church is involvement in cross-cultural engagement of the gospel.

While much of the rest of the world is embracing the gospel in increasing numbers, many in the West are running away from God (or at least what they believe God is), and in particular Jesus Christ, as fast as they can. But this trend in the West does not need to continue. We can return to the cultural foundations which made us great. Loren Cunningham puts it well:

While Western nations fear the increase of Islam in Europe, they seem blind to the greater problem – the loss of their own faith. If we in the West continue to deny God's relevance, or even His existence, and especially if we continue to turn away from the absolute truths revealed in the Bible, our leadership will decline. Our cultures will turn more and more to pleasure seeking, materialism, irresponsibility, dishonesty, corruption

138. Walls (2002) p67-69

and violence. We will descend into poverty. Like Judah in the reign of King Manasseh, America and the West will crumble. And if China continues its phenomenal church growth, it will become the new leader within three or four generations.

However, I do not believe the West has to decline. We can see both China and the West – and all the nations of the world – rise to the potential God has instilled in every land. We can even see the West and China living in peace and unity, serving the same God. We can see our countries turned around; we can see our foundations restored. And those foundations rest in one book – God's book.[139]

---

139. Cunningham (2007, p. 27)

To study and discuss

1. How are you, personally, involved in cross-cultural engagement of the gospel? (Remember this does not have to be overseas – it could well be with the person next door)

2. Can you explain the gospel of Jesus without using the 'in-words' of the Christian community?

3. Are you open to the scrutiny and advice of others?
- Have you personally or your church corporately asked a brother or sister in the Lord from a different culture to appraise your practice?
- What sort of thing do you think you could learn from doing this?

To Pray

Pray for the second generation of believers in countries such as Korea:
- That they will not become just cultural Christians
- That they will not be lured by the affluence that has come with the Kingdom principles in the nation
- That they will personally engage with the Lord
- That they will be involved in cross-cultural communication of the Gospel.

CULTURE FOR ETERNITY

EIGHTEEN

The Ultimate Glorious Unity in Diversity

On one of His journeys from Judea to Galilee, Jesus deliberately travelled through Samaria. True to form, He got into deep conversation with someone other than a Jewish man. When the conversation got too revealingly personal, the Samaritan woman raised the topic of the mountain at which people should worship. The Samaritans had chosen the tradition of worshiping God at Mt Gerizim, the mountain of blessing since the days of Joshua. Jesus' reply was revealing.

> Believe me, woman, a time is coming when you will worship the Father neither on this mountain nor in Jerusalem. You Samaritans worship what you do not know: we worship what we do know, for salvation is from the Jews. Yet a time is coming and has now come when true worshipers will worship the Father in spirit and truth, for they are the kind of worshipers the Father seeks.[140]

Jesus clearly was telling her that what counts is not the place of worship. This is a cultural form. What matters is that the worship is informed by true revelation and is from the heart – in spirit and truth. What counts is the right object of worship and the heart attitude. The ways in which this can be expressed are diverse. Jesus said

---

140. John 4:21-23

this was the way it was to be both now and in the future.

Various parts of scripture speak of the people of God coming into maturity, the unity and fullness of Christ. Notably Colossians and Ephesians speak of our fullness in Christ and our coming into the fullness of Christ. The source of our unity and completeness is Christ Himself.

For in Christ all the fullness of the Deity lives in bodily form, and you have been given fullness in Christ, who is the head over every power and authority.[141]

God's original purpose for us was to be bearers of His image, to reflect His fullness, the fullness of the Trinity, the unity and diversity found in God Himself. There is no way that just one of us could reflect anything like a significant part of His glory. One person, one community or one people group would be totally inadequate. We will only adequately reflect something of His multiple layers of beauty and multiple aspects of glory when we come together in all our diversity and in perfect unity.

The means of our unity and completeness is the grace of God through the work of Christ on the cross. Without the work of Christ bringing us together we will remain in ugly disunity, not appreciating the magnificence of His diversity expressed in our diversity. Without the grace of God we remain lost as children of anger, separated from each other because we are separated from God. But He has made us alive together with Him, and elevated us together in the heavenlies in Christ. We were aliens and strangers but now we are one in Him, different in culture but one in relationship with Him. He is our peace. He has placed us in one household. We are brothers and sisters, children of God.[142]

---

141. Colossians 2:9,10
142. Ephesians 2

The complete fulfilment of our unity and completeness will happen when we all come together in the unity of the faith and the knowledge of Him and the perfection of humanity.[143]

This process is not an end in itself, but rather "in order that in the coming ages he might show the incomparable riches of his grace, expressed in his kindness to us in Christ Jesus".[144] Millions of us in all our diversity of cultural groups – communities, languages, people groups and nations will bring resounding glory to God.[145]

After this I looked and there before me was a great multitude that no-one could count, from every nation, people and language, standing before the throne and in front of the Lamb ... and they cried in a loud voice: "Salvation belongs to our God, who sits on the throne, and to the Lamb"... "Amen, Praise and glory and wisdom and thanks and honour and power and strength be to our God forever and ever. Amen!"[146]

Diversity of culture always has and always will matter to God. God's original intention for the human race, to reflect His glory in His unity and diversity, will be complete in our united and diverse worship of Him.

What a glorious prospect! It makes me salivate in anticipation. I can't wait! Or, as the book of Revelation puts it, "Amen. Come, Lord Jesus."

---

143. Ephesians 4
144. Ephesians 2:7
145. Revelation 5:9
146. Revelation 7:9-12

To do

1. Draw a continuum line across a large page. On one end write 'deepest' and the other end 'most superficial'. On this line place your relationship with God and all the features of a culture which are part of your life. Include all or most of those found on the diagrams in chapter one. Now examine your life honestly.

- Where is the major focus of your life?
- How do the other features connect to your major focus and serve the main thing?
- Prayerfully examine your heart and ask the Lord if He would have you make changes.

2. Get out of your comfort zone and go and worship the Lord using the forms of a totally different culture!

Get used to it. You might be spending eternity discovering new ways to worship Him, like discovering new types of food, as you discover more and more fantastic dimensions of God's glorious person and character.

References

Carson, D. A. (2008). *Christ and culture revisited.* Grand Rapids, MI: Eerdmans.

Cunningham, L., & Rogers, J. (2007). *The book that transforms nations, The power of the Bible to change any country.* Seattle: YWAM.

Flannagan, M. (1999). The left is not right, *Reality Magazine,* 35 available: http://www.reality.org.nz/articles/35/35-flannagan.php,

Latourette, K. S. (1937). *A history of the expansion of Christianity.* New York: Harper & Brothers Publishers.

McDonald, G. (2008). *Young lions.* Southport Park, QLD: METRO Church Australia Ltd

Niebuhr, H. R. (1951). *Christ and culture.* New York: Harper Torchbooks.

Newbigin, L. (1986). *Foolishness to the Greeks: The gospel and western culture.* Grand Rapids: Eerdmans.

Olsen, B. E. (1978). *Bruchko.* Illinois: Creation House Carole Strum.

Rentoul, J. (1997). *Tony Blair.* London: Warner Books.

Richardson, D. (1981). *Eternity in their hearts.* Ventura, CA: Regal Books.

Schaeffer, F. A. (1976). *How should we then live? The rise and decline of western thought and culture.* Wheaton Illinois: Crossway Books.

Stott, J. (1984). *Issues facing Christians today.* Basingskote, UK: Marshall, Morgan & Scott.

Trebilco, P. (2006). Gospel, culture, and the public sphere: Perspectives from the New Testament. *Evangel, 24*(2), 37-45.

Turner, H. (2001). *Frames of mind: a public philosophy for religions and cultures.* Auckland, NZ: The DeepSight Trust.

Walls, A. F. (2002). *The cross-cultural process in Christian history.* New York: Orbis Books.

Watkins, C. (2008). Discovering a theology for the Christian teacher today. *Journal of Education and Christian Belief, 12*(1), 53-68.

www.ingramcontent.com/pod-product-compliance
Lightning Source LLC
Chambersburg PA
CBHW072134020426
42334CB00018B/1797